The
COMPANIONS *in Christ*™

Durham

Network™

www.companionsinchrist.org

So much more!

Companions in Christ offers *so much more* than printed resources. It offers an ongoing LEADERSHIP NETWORK that provides:

- ➤ Opportunities to connect with other churches who are also journeying through the *Companions in Christ* series.
- ➤ Helpful leadership tips and articles as well as updated lists of supplemental resources
- ➤ Training opportunities that develop and deepen the leadership skills used in formational groups
- ➤ An online discussion room where you can share or gather information
- ➤ Insights and testimonies from other *Companions in Christ* leaders
- ➤ FREE *Companions in Christ* posters to use as you promote the group in your congregation

Just complete this form and drop it in the mail, and you can enjoy the many benefits available through the Companions in Christ NETWORK! Or, enter your contact information at www.companionsinchrist.org/leaders.

- ❑ Add my name to the *Companions in Christ* NETWORK email list so that I can receive ongoing information about small-group resources and leadership trainings
- ❑ Please send me FREE *Companions in Christ* posters. Indicate quantity needed: (Also available online.)

Name: _____

Address: _____

City/State/Zip: _____

Church: _____

Email: _____

Phone: _____

D1308022

COMPANIONS *in Christ*

Upper Room Ministries
PO Box 340012
Nashville, TN 37203-9540

COMPANIONS *in Christ*

A SMALL-GROUP EXPERIENCE IN SPIRITUAL FORMATION

The Way of PRAYER

Leader's Guide

Marjorie J. Thompson

UPPER ROOM BOOKS®

NASHVILLE

Cover design: Left Coast Design, Portland, Oregon
Cover photograph: jupiterimages.com
First printing: 2006

Library of Congress Cataloging-in-Publication Data

Thompson, Marjorie J., 1953–
   Companions in Christ: the way of prayer leader's guide / Marjorie J. Thompson
       p. cm.
  ISBN-13: 978-0-8358-9907-9
  ISBN-10: 0-8358-9906-1
  1. Prayer—Christianity—Study and teaching. I. Title.
BV215.T49 2007
253'.7—dc22
2006023056

Printed in the United States of America.

For more information on *Companions in Christ,*
visit www.companionsinchrist.org or call 1-800-972-0433.

Contents

Acknowledgments   5

Introduction   7

Weekly Needs at a Glance   17

Preparatory Meeting   21

Week 1   How Do You Pray?   31

Week 2   Images of God   37

Week 3   Praying by Heart   43

Week 4   Praying with Music   49

Week 5   Praying by Gaze   53

Week 6   Praying with Our Bodies   59

Week 7   Scriptural Prayer   65

Week 8   Contemplative Prayer   71

Week 9   Praying with and for Others   77

Week 10   Prayer and Social Transformation   81

Notes   87

Evaluation   89

About the Author   91

Acknowledgments

The original twenty-eight week *Companions in Christ* resource grew from the seeds of a vision long held by Stephen D. Bryant, editor and publisher of Upper Room Ministries. It was given shape by Marjorie J. Thompson, director of Pathways in Congregational Spirituality with Upper Room Ministries and spiritual director to *Companions in Christ*. The vision, which has now expanded into the Companions in Christ series, was realized through the efforts of many people over many years. The original advisers, consultants, authors, editors, and test churches are acknowledged in the foundational twenty-eight week resource. We continue to owe an immense debt of gratitude to each person and congregation named there.

The Way of Prayer is the seventh title in the Companions in Christ series. The original twenty-eight-week resource was intended as a foundation for small groups who want to explore the journey of spiritual formation together. Several resources have been developed for groups who want to continue their communities of spiritual formation and growth. Those resources include *The Way of Grace*, *The Way of Blessedness*, *The Way of Forgiveness*, and *The Way of Transforming Discipleship*. Recently *Exploring the Way* was released as a basic introduction to spiritual formation for groups of all sizes, offering a taste of the Companions in Christ series.

The resource you hold in your hand, *The Way of Prayer*, is intended as a follow-up for the original twenty-eight-week resource but may also be used prior to it. If this is the first *Companions* resource your small group is using, it may create a hunger for ongoing formational experiences in community that the other books in the series could help facilitate. If so, we highly recommend the twenty-eight-week *Companions in Christ* resource.

The articles in *The Way of Prayer* were written by Jane E. Vennard. The daily exercises in the Participant's Book are primarily the work of Stephen D. Bryant and Susanna Southard, based on early suggestions by Jane Vennard. The Deeper Explorations in the Leader's Guide are primarily the work of Marjorie Thompson in consultation with Jane Vennard. The work of the whole benefited from input by an editorial team of the *Companions in Christ* staff, including Stephen Bryant, Lynne Deming, and Kathleen Stephens. Special thanks go to three members of the Companions Advisory Board: Janet Salyer, Schuyler Bissell, and Mark Wilson, who read and responded to drafts of the material.

Introduction

Welcome to *Companions in Christ: The Way of Prayer*, a small-group resource designed to help your group explore and experience the great variety of prayer paths available to us in the Christian tradition. Many people feel inadequate when it comes to prayer or find that their upbringing has offered limited ways of understanding and practicing prayer. This resource aims to help expand both mind and heart in relation to perhaps the most central of all spiritual disciplines. *The Way of Prayer* will help members of your group examine their personal history with prayer and their ideas about God. It will then enable them to experiment with a broad array of practices that can help them integrate prayer into the whole of their lives.

In response to small groups who want to continue their exploration of spiritual practices that began with the original twenty-eight-week *Companions in Christ* resource, the Companions in Christ series continues to expand. *The Way of Prayer* is the seventh in the series. Earlier titles in the series are *The Way of Forgiveness, The Way of Blessedness, The Way of Grace, Exploring the Way,* and *The Way of Transforming Discipleship.*

With the exception of *Exploring the Way*, each resource in the Companions series expands on the foundational content of the twenty-eight-week resource and uses the same basic format. Using a different format, *Exploring the Way* introduces spiritual practice. The foundational resource, *Companions in Christ,* explores the Christian spiritual life under five headings: Journey, Scripture, Prayer, Call, and Spiritual Guidance. Most supplementary volumes of the Companions in Christ series explore in greater depth some aspect of one of these primary categories of spiritual practice.

The Way of Prayer clearly falls under the Prayer heading, as it expands on prayer practices that enable us to sustain lifelong Christian discipleship. As in previous *Companions* resources, the approach to scripture is more formational than informational. Scripture is central to the resource, but this is not a traditional Bible study. We will focus on how various passages touch our hearts, move our wills, and shape our spirits to conform more fully to the life of Christ.

About the Resource and Process

Like all resources in the Companions in Christ series, *The Way of Prayer* has two primary components: (1) individual reading and daily exercises throughout the week in the Participant's Book and (2) a weekly two-hour meeting based on directions in the Leader's Guide. The Participant's Book has a weekly article that introduces new material and five daily exercises to help participants reflect on their lives in light of the article's content. These exercises help participants move from *information* (knowledge about) to *experience* (knowledge of). An important part of this process involves keeping a personal notebook or journal in which participants record reflections, prayers, and questions for later review and for reference at the weekly group meeting. The daily exercise commitment is about thirty minutes. The weekly meeting includes time for reflecting on the past week's exercises, for moving into deeper experiences of spiritual growth, and for engaging in group experiences of worship.

The material in *The Way of Prayer* includes a preparatory meeting followed by ten weekly sessions. Following is a brief overview of the content of the sessions.

1. *How Do You Pray?:* Examining our personal histories with prayer, raising the possibility of greater variety in our practice, and hearing God's call to deeper relationship.

2. *Images of God:* Reexamining our positive and negative images of God, with an exploration of alternative images based on Jesus' life and teachings.

3. *Praying by Heart:* Introducing the ancient Jesus Prayer and related forms of prayer of the heart for today, including use of the Psalms.

4. *Praying with Music:* Discovering, listening to, and making music as expressions of prayer and opening ourselves to new genres of music as vehicles of prayer.

5. *Praying by Gaze:* Exploring the nature of gazing, encountering the place of icons in Eastern Orthodox prayer, and exploring gaze as a sensory vehicle for our prayer practice.

6. *Praying with Our Bodies:* Acknowledging anxieties about the body; recognizing how our bodies already participate in prayer; and giving ourselves permission to explore embodied prayer in gesture, posture, and action.

7. *Scriptural Prayer:* Affirming the central place of scripture in shaping our prayer, and offering two major paths of scriptural prayer and meditation. Includes section on examen, or self-examination.

8. *Contemplative Prayer*: Describing "the way of mystery" in Christian prayer, introducing Centering Prayer and discernment, and encouraging contemplative prayer in the midst of ordinary life.

9. *Praying with and for Others*: Acknowledging the necessity of Christian community in prayer, and encouraging various expressions of prayer with and for one another.

10. *Prayer and Social Transformation*: Connecting prayer with the social order and reinforcing its role in bringing about transformation according to God's will.

The Companions in Christ Network

The *Companions in Christ* Network provides a place for sharing conversation and information. The *Companions* Web site, www.companionsinchrist.org, includes a discussion room where you can offer insights, voice questions, and respond to others in an ongoing process of shared learning. Please visit the Web site for further information on *Companions* training events.

The Role of the Small-Group Leader

Leading a group for spiritual formation differs in many ways from teaching a class. The most obvious difference is in your basic goal as group leader. In a class, you have particular information (facts, theories, ways of doing things) that you want to convey. You can gauge your success at the end of the class by how well participants demonstrate some grasp of the information. In a group for spiritual formation, your goal is to enable spiritual growth in each group member. You work in partnership with the Holy Spirit, who alone can bring about transformation of the human heart. Here gaining wisdom is more important than gaining knowledge, and growing in holiness is more important than gaining either knowledge or wisdom. Success, if that word has any meaning in this context, will be evident over months and even years in the changed lives of group members.

Classes tend to be task-oriented. Groups for spiritual formation tend to be more process-oriented. Even though group members will have done common preparation in reading and daily exercises, group discussions may move in directions you do not expect. You will need to be open to the movement of the Holy Spirit and vigilant in discerning the difference between following the Spirit's lead and going off on a tangent. Such discernment requires careful, prayerful listening—a far more important skill for a group leader than talking.

Finally, classes primarily focus on a set of objective data: a Bible passage, information from a book, or analyses of current events. A group for spiritual formation, however, focuses on the personal faith experience of each group member. Each person seeks to understand and be open to the grace and revelation of God. When group members have read and reflected on a scripture passage, the basis for group discussion is not "What did the author intend to say to readers of that time?" but "How does this passage connect to my life or illuminate my experience?" Discussion centers around a sharing of experience, not a debate over ideas. You will model this type of personal sharing with your group because of your involvement in all parts of the group meeting. The type of leadership needed differs from that of a traditional church school teacher or small-group facili-tator. As leader, you will read the material and complete the daily exercises along with other members and bring your responses to share with the group. You will lead by offering your honest reflections and by enabling the group members to listen carefully to one another and to the Spirit in your midst.

Leading a group for spiritual formation requires particular qualities. Foremost among these are patience and trust. You will need patience to allow the sessions to unfold as they will. Spiritual formation is a lifelong process. Identifying visible personal growth in group members over the course of *The Way of Prayer* may be difficult. It may take a while for group members to adjust to the purpose and style of a formational group process. As a group leader, resolve to ask questions with no "right" answers in mind and to encourage participants to talk about their own experiences. Setting an example of sharing your experience rather than proclaiming abstract truths or talking about the experiences of other well-known Christians will accelerate this shift from an informational approach to a formational process. Trust that the Holy Spirit will indeed help group members to see or hear what they really need. You may offer what you consider a great insight to which no one responds. If it is what the group needs, the Spirit will bring it around again at a more opportune time. Susan Muto, a modern writer on spiritual formation, often says that we need to "make space for the pace of grace." There are no shortcuts to spiritual growth. Be patient and trust the Spirit.

Listening is another critical quality for a leader of a spiritual formation group. This does not mean simply listening for people to say what you hope they will say so you can reinforce them. Listen for what is actually going on in participants' minds and hearts, which may differ from what you expect after reading the material and doing the weekly exercises yourself. While you listen, jot down brief notes about themes that surface. Does sharing center around a particular type of experience? Is a certain direction or common understanding emerging—a hint of God's will or a shared sense of what group members found helpful? What do you hear again and again? What action might group members take together or individually to respond to an emerging sense of call?

A group leader also needs to be accepting. Accept that group members may have had spiritual experiences quite unlike yours and that people often see common experiences in different ways. Some may be struck by an aspect that did not impress you at all, while others may be left cold by dimensions that really move you. As you model acceptance, you help foster acceptance of differences within the group. Beyond accepting differences, you will need to accept lack of closure. Group meetings rarely tie up all the loose ends in a neat package. Burning questions will be left hanging. You can trust the Spirit to bring resolution in time, if resolution is needed. Also be prepared to accept people's emotions along with their thoughts and experiences. Tears, fears, joy, and anger are legitimate responses along this journey. One important expression of acceptance is permission-giving. Permit group members to grow and share at their own pace. Let them know in your first meeting that while you encourage full participation in every part of the process, they are free to opt out of anything that makes them feel uncomfortable. No one will be forced to share or pray without consent. "Where the Spirit of the Lord is, there is freedom" (2 Cor. 3:17).

It is particularly important to avoid three common tendencies:

1. *Fixing.* When someone presents a specific problem, you may be tempted to find a solution and "fix" the problem. Problem solving generally makes you feel better. Perhaps it makes you feel wise or helps to break the tension, but it will not help the other to grow. Moreover, you might prescribe the wrong fix. If you have faced a similar problem, speak only from your own experience.

2. *Proselytizing.* You know what has brought you closer to God. Naturally you would like everyone to try it. You can offer your own experience to the group but trying to convince others to follow your path is spiritually dangerous. Here is where your knowledge and wisdom come into play. Teresa of Ávila wrote that if she had to choose between a director who was spiritual and one who was learned, she would pick the learned one. The saint might be able to talk only about his or her own spiritual path. The learned one might at least recognize another person's experience from having read about it. Clarifying and celebrating someone else's experience is far more useful than urging others to try to follow your way.

3. *Controlling.* Many of us are accustomed to filling in silence with comment. You may be tempted to think you should have an appropriate response to whatever anyone says; that is, you may tend to dominate and control the conversation. Here again, patience and listening are essential. Do not be afraid of silence. Your capacity to be comfortable with silence allows you to be a relaxed presence in the group. If you cannot bear a long silence, break it with an invitation for someone (maybe one who has been quiet so far) to share a thought, feeling, or question rather than with a comment of your own.

If this style of leadership seems challenging or unfamiliar to you, consider attending a leader training event for *Companions in Christ*. While leadership training is not required to use this resource, it is recommended and encouraged.

Expectations for the Opening and Sharing Insights Sections of Meetings

This section offers a basic process for the first hour of your group session. The first step in the group session is prayer and a time of quiet centering. Invoking the Holy Spirit's guiding presence is especially important in the Opening portion of the weekly group meeting (see "A General Outline for Group Meetings," pages 14–16).

Most of the Sharing Insights part of the group session will focus on individual members discussing their experiences with the daily exercises. Members should bring their journals to refresh their memories of the week's exercises. As the leader, you will want to begin with your own reflections, which sets the tone for the rest of the group. Speak briefly (two to three minutes) in order to allow ample time for others to share. Above all, specifically relate one of your responses to a daily exercise. If your sharing is general or abstract, other participants will be less likely to share personal experiences. Your initial offering in this part of the group meeting is one of your most important roles as a leader. Consider carefully each week what you would like to say, remaining mindful of the role your words can play in establishing group trust and the serious intent of this part of the meeting.

You may also describe and model for the group an approach sometimes called "sharing to the center." The Christ candle set in the middle of the group affirms that Christ is truly the center of all that the group members do and say in the meeting. The living Christ, through the presence of the Holy Spirit, mediates personal sharing. Therefore, participants can share with one another in God's presence by visually focusing on the candle. This focus lessens the need to keep constant eye contact with other participants, which makes revealing deeply personal responses less difficult. The practice also helps the group to sense that God is truly the one with healing answers and guiding solutions, not us.

During the Sharing Insights time, your main job is to listen. Listen primarily for themes—similar experiences that suggest a general truth about the spiritual life, common responses to the readings that might indicate a word God wants the group to hear, or experiences that might offer practical help to other group members as they try to hear and respond to God's call. Take notes so you can lift up these themes as the Sharing Insights time comes to an end. You will also ask other group members to share any themes or patterns they may have identified from the discussion. Listen too for key differences in participants' experiences and affirm the variety of ways God speaks to and guides each one of us. Be alert to participants' temptation to fix problems, control conversation, or proselytize. Gently remind them to share only their own experiences or responses. The same guidance applies if a participant mentions someone else, whether in the group or outside it, as an example. Nothing can destroy group trust more quickly than exposing confidences.

By establishing up front some ground rules for group sharing, you may avoid problems. In the Preparatory Meeting, you will explain the various components of each week's meeting. Discuss the nature of this sharing time and establish some basic ground rules for the group. Here are some suggestions:

- Speak only for yourself about beliefs, feelings, and responses.
- Respect and receive what others offer, even if you disagree.
- Listen more than talk. Avoid "cross talk"—interrupting, speaking for others, or trying to fix another person's problems.
- Honor the different ways God works in individuals.
- Do not be afraid of silence. Use it to listen to the Spirit in your midst.
- Maintain confidentiality. What is shared in the group stays in the group. If spouses or close friends are in the same group, they will want to establish outside of meeting time mutually agreeable boundaries to their personal sharing in the group.
- Recognize that all group members have permission to share only what and when they are ready to share.
- Group members have permission to opt out of a process but not to belittle it aloud.

You may want to add to this list before you discuss it with the group.

A few minutes before the scheduled end of the Sharing Insights time, state aloud any themes you have noted: a summary report on what you have heard, not a chance to get in the last word. Make it fairly brief: "I noticed that several of us were drawn to a particular passage. I wonder if God is trying to call our attention to something here." This is a time for summarizing and tying together themes that have already surfaced.

Finally, you may want to close this part of the session with prayer for the deepening of particular insights, for the ability to follow through on the themes or guidance you have heard, for God's leading on questions that have been left open, or for particular situations that have been mentioned. And you may want to invite all group members who are willing to offer simple sentence prayers of their own.

A General Outline for Group Meetings

The weekly group meetings will typically follow the outline explained below. Within the outline are two overall movements: one emphasizes sharing insights and learnings from the week's reading and daily exercises; the other develops a deeper understanding of spiritual disciplines or practices. The first movement, Sharing Insights, is described in the preceding section. The second part of the meeting, called Deeper Explorations, may expand on ideas contained in the week's reading, offer practice in spiritual exercises related to the week's theme, or give participants time to reflect on the implications of what they have learned for their own journeys and for the church. It may include a brief look forward if special preparation is needed for the coming week.

Both movements are intended as times for formation. The first focuses on the group members' responses to the weekly reading and exercises. The second focuses on expanding and deepening the week's theme experientially. Some participants may respond more readily to one part of the weekly meeting than the other. For example, one person may write pages of journal responses to the daily exercises and be eager for the Sharing Insights time but express reticence in joining a group process for the Deeper Explorations. Another person who has had difficulty reflecting on daily exercises may have little to say during the Sharing Insights time but receive great energy and joy from participating in an experiential learning process. Such variations of response may reflect personality types, while other differences may reflect circumstances or life stages in a person's journey. Be patient, accepting, and encouraging of the fullest level of participation each group member can offer.

Consider carefully the setting for your group meetings. An adaptable space enhances group process. One helpful arrangement is a circle of comfortable chairs or sofas. Or participants might want a surface for writing or drawing. Since the group will sometimes break into pairs or triads, plenty of room to separate is also important. Choose a space for meeting that is relatively quiet and peaceful.

A visual focus for the group is important, especially for opening and closing worship times. Some weeks you are free to create this focus in whatever way you choose, perhaps simply with a candle on a small table in the center of the circle.

OPENING (10–15 MINUTES)

This brief time of worship will give group members a chance to quiet down and prepare for the group session to follow. Each group will eventually discover what works best for its members. This Leader's Guide offers specific suggestions; but if you desire, you can develop your own pattern of prayer and centering. Possibilities for this opening worship include (1) singing a hymn together or listening to a selected song on audiotape or CD; (2) silence; (3) lighting a candle; (4) scripture or other reading; (5) individual prayer, planned or extemporaneous; or (6) group prayer using a written or memorized prayer.

SHARING INSIGHTS (40–45 MINUTES)

The content for this part of the meeting comes from the weekly reading and from participants' responses to the five daily exercises they have completed since the last meeting. If members fail to read the material or skip the daily exercises, they will be left out. If too many come unprepared, the group process simply will not work. Group interaction will generally follow the model given above under "Expectations for the Opening and Sharing Insights Sections of Meetings." Since the Opening has provided prayer and centering time, this section begins with sharing from you as the group leader, continues with group interaction, and ends with a summary, followed by a brief prayer. You will need to keep an eye on the time in order to bring the sharing to a close and have time for the summary and prayer.

BREAK (10 MINUTES)

Group break time serves important physical, mental, and relational purposes. It also offers a chance for snacking if you choose to do that. If so, arrange for someone to provide food. Do not neglect this break time, and be sure to take a break yourself as leader.

DEEPER EXPLORATIONS (45 MINUTES)

This part of the group meeting builds on material in the weekly reading and daily exercises. The content is designed to help group members explore in greater depth the weekly theme, generally through scriptural meditation, prayer, creative process, personal reflection, and sharing. This segment of the meeting resembles the experiential part of a spiritual retreat in miniature and requires thoughtful preparation if you are to guide the process comfortably. Review the leader material early in the week prior to the meeting so that you have time to think through the process, complete any preparation, and gather materials.

CLOSING (10 MINUTES)

As it began, the group meeting ends with a brief time of worship. First you may need to attend to practical matters of the next session's meeting place or provision of refreshments if these vary from week to week. You may also have the group draw names for prayer partners for the coming week and ask for prayer requests.

This guide includes specific suggestions for the Closing. Designed to follow closely the Deeper Explorations, they may include symbolic acts or rituals of celebration and commitment.

Concluding Matters

Song or hymn selections for the Opening and Closing times need careful consideration. Review the hymnals or songbooks available to you, and look for singable tunes with thematically appropriate words. If your group sings reluctantly, locate several audiocassette tapes or CDs to play and invite sing-alongs or simply enjoy listening.

This Leader's Guide suggests songs for each meeting. A number of these come from a songbook titled *The Faith We Sing* (TFWS), published by Abingdon Press. This recommended resource is ecumenical in scope. It contains songs that represent several worship styles; it is small, portable, and easy to obtain. Most songs in it are simple and singable. Abingdon Press now offers a CD with musical accompaniment to every song in the book. We encourage your group to consider this music resource, while recognizing that each group will have access to different songbooks and may have its own preference. Some songs are referenced from *The United Methodist Hymnal* (UMH), though they can be found in many hymnals. Another excellent resource now available is the new *Upper Room Worshipbook* (URWB).

The purpose of the Companions in Christ series is to equip persons of faith with both personal and corporate spiritual life practices that will continue long beyond the time frame of any particular resource. Participants may continue certain disciplines on their own or carry some practices into congregational life. Others may desire to continue meeting as a small group. As you guide your group through this journey, you may discover that certain subjects or practices generate interest and energy for further exploration. Some group members may wish that certain readings or weekly meetings could go into more depth. When the group expresses strong desire to continue with a particular topic or practice, take note of it. A number of possibilities exist for small-group study and practice beyond this resource. Some suggested resources are listed on pages 137–140 of the Participant's Book. The group will need to decide future directions toward the end of this experience.

Our prayer for you as a leader is that the weeks ahead will lead you and your group deeper into the gracious mystery of prayer in all its splendid and varied expressions. May your explorations lead you deeper into communion with the heart of God, where you will find yourselves connected in vital compassion to the world God so loves. May your companionship with Christ and with one another be richly blessed!

Weekly Needs at a Glance

Review this Weekly Needs at a Glance list to familiarize yourself with items needed at *The Way of Prayer* Preparatory Meeting and the other weekly meetings. Knowing well in advance the items required for each meeting will help you avoid last-minute crises.

Weekly Materials

ALL MEETINGS

- Christ candle (large white pillar candle) or other central candle
- table, covered with a cloth
- matches or lighter
- hymnals, songbooks, or other arrangements for music (audiocassettes/CDs and player); several options are suggested each week from which you may choose for Opening and Closing
- extra Bibles
- sheets of blank paper, pens or pencils
- bell or chime
- group ground rules developed during your preparatory meeting, printed on newsprint and posted in your meeting room
- newsprint and markers or chalkboard/whiteboard
- Candle Prayer, printed on newsprint and posted in your meeting room (if you choose to use the following prayer as a group):

> *Light of Christ*
> *Shine on our path*
> *Chase away all darkness*
> *and lead us to the heart of God.*
> *Amen.*

PREPARATORY MEETING

- copy of the Participant's Book for each person
- copies of the Companions *Journal* for those who may wish to purchase one
- marker and newsprint (or flipchart) with group ground rules written out in advance
- copy of "Holy Listening Exercise" (page 28) and "Review Questions" (page 29) for each participant
- the card "Prayers for Our Way of Prayer Group" (in the back of this Leader's Guide)
- hymns or songs for the Opening and Closing

WEEK 1: HOW DO YOU PRAY?

- copy of "My Personal History with Prayer" (page 36) for each participant

WEEK 2: IMAGES OF GOD

- preprinted newsprint sheet with divine names/images from scripture (see Daily Exercises 2 and 3)
- preprinted newsprint sheet with divine names/images from select hymns
- list of names for God for the Closing prayer
- copy of *The Faith We Sing* and "Bring Many Names" (TFWS #2047)

WEEK 4: PRAYING WITH MUSIC

- CD or audiocassette tape of music from Exercise 2
- a selection of music to play for the Opening or recorded accompaniment
- masking tape (if using newsprint)
- symbols of music for worship center

WEEK 5: PRAYING BY GAZE

- icon or other picture of Christ (check your local religious bookstores)

- photo of a loved one
- photo of a stranger
- table, covered with a cloth
- four or five votive candles
- one large poster board
- glue stick or double-sided tape

WEEK 6: PRAYING WITH OUR BODIES

- four scripture texts from Deeper Explorations written on folded paper or card stock
- tape or backing to post scripture texts at each posture station
- selected psalm or Lord's Prayer for reading
- copy of "Sacred the Body" from *The Faith We Sing* (TFWS #2228)
- basket containing small stones, pocket crosses, wrist/finger strings, tea candles (an assortment from which each participant may choose an item)
- digital or instant camera (optional)

WEEK 7: SCRIPTURAL PRAYER

- copy of reflection sheet on Ezekiel 37 for each participant
- small dry twigs or sticks
- small bowl of water and a floating candle or fresh flower

WEEK 8: CONTEMPLATIVE PRAYER

- recorded instrumental music

WEEK 9: PRAYING WITH AND FOR OTHERS

- anointing oil

WEEK 10: PRAYER AND SOCIAL TRANSFORMATION

- drawing materials for group mandala process
- blank paper, colored pencils/markers, scissors, glue sticks, magazine pictures of human and natural interest that depict situations or images related to peaceful human community, economic health, and ecological vitality

- large circle of heavy paper or cardboard (at least four feet in diameter) marked with enough wedges for each participant, leaving a small empty circle at the center (six to eight inches)
- round or square table for mandala process and space for art supplies

Preparatory Meeting

The Leader's Guide to *Companions in Christ: The Way of Prayer* directly addresses you, the leader, as it presents the material for each group meeting. In places the Leader's Guide offers suggested words for you to speak to the group as a way of introducing various sections. Where this occurs, the words are printed in a bold typeface (such as the first item under "Set a context"). These words are only suggestions. Feel free to express the same idea in your own words or to adapt as you deem necessary. Remember to speak at a deliberate pace. Whether giving instructions or offering prayers, not rushing your words communicates a sense of peace and grace.

When instructed to guide a reflection process, you will often see ellipses (...). These marks indicate pauses between your sentences to allow participants to ponder them. You will need to develop your own sense of timing in relation to the overall time frame for the guided meditation. Generally fifteen to thirty seconds are sufficient for each pause. In some cases, the text will recommend specific times for certain pauses.

The Leader's Guide assumes that groups are new to the *Companions in Christ* resources and provides complete explanation of all aspects of the journey. For example, in the Preparatory Meeting participants carefully review the daily and weekly rhythm and are introduced to the printed resource. If your entire group has experienced *Companions*, feel free to abbreviate familiar material and focus on this resource's distinctive aspects and your group's process. One exception is the "Holy Listening Exercise," which is part of this Preparatory Meeting. A review of deep listening, central to spiritual formation, can benefit even an experienced group. Upper Room Ministries encourages leaders to include this experience.

PREPARATION

Prepare yourself spiritually. Review the Introduction to the Participant's Book for *The Way of Prayer*, as well as the Introduction in this Leader's Guide. Look over the Contents page in the

Participant's Book so you can answer basic questions about weekly topics. Pray for your newly forming group and for each of the participants by name. Ask God's guidance as you lead and for each group member as together you embark on this spiritual journey.

Prepare materials and the meeting space.

- Set up chairs in a circle with a small center table and Christ candle. Make your meeting space inviting and visually attractive.
- Have a copy of the Participant's Book for each person and several copies of the *Companions Journal* for those who may wish to purchase one.
- You will need a marker and flipchart (or newsprint) with group ground rules written out in advance.
- Provide the card "Prayers for Our *Way of Prayer* Group" (in the back of this Leader's Guide).
- You will need copies of the handouts titled "Holy Listening Exercise" (page 28) and "Review Questions" (page 29) for each participant.
- Choose hymns or songs for the Opening and Closing, and secure hymnals or songbooks.

Review the intent of this meeting: To gain a clear grasp of the purpose and process of *The Way of Prayer*, to provide an opportunity to ask questions and express hopes for the journey, to begin getting acquainted with the group, and to review and adopt group ground rules.

OPENING (10 MINUTES)

Welcome all participants by name as they enter. Be sure that each participant has a copy of the Participant's Book for *The Way of Prayer* and a journal or a notebook.

Set a context.

- This meeting will prepare us for a wonderful ten-week journey of exploration into one of the greatest of all spiritual practices, prayer.
- *The Way of Prayer*, like all the *Companions in Christ* resources, is a small-group experience in spiritual formation. The larger purpose is to give the Holy Spirit time and space to shape us into greater Christlikeness.
- Prayer is one of the great privileges of the Christian life. God has given us freedom to reach out in faith and hope to the power of divine love. In prayer we connect with the grace and mystery of God.
- But often we don't feel we know how best to pray or just what to pray for. Most of us sense that there could be more to our prayer life. *The Way of Prayer* will help us expand

our understanding of prayer and explore a variety of ways to pray. It will help us integrate prayer more fully into the whole of our lives.

Provide a brief overview of the Preparatory Meeting.
— A chance for group members to introduce themselves
— Opening worship similar to what they will experience in each weekly meeting
— Discussion of the group process
— Discussion of group members' responsibilities
— An experience in "Holy Listening"
— Closing worship similar to what they will experience in each weekly meeting

Ask participants to introduce themselves.
- Ask participants to introduce themselves by saying their name and a few words about what drew them to this group.
- As leader, model by introducing yourself first. Keep your comments brief and simple to encourage others to do likewise.

Join together in worship.
- Invite the group into a spirit of worship. Light the Christ candle and indicate that you will begin each meeting this way to acknowledge the presence of the risen Lord in your midst. Offer words to this effect: **Living Christ, we light this candle trusting your real presence in our time together this day. Help us open ourselves to your spirit of grace and guidance as we begin our exploration of** *The Way of Prayer* **together.**
- Read Psalm 89:1-2. Allow a few moments of quiet to let people absorb the words. Then use the following words or ones of your own: **God's steadfast love draws us to prayer, and God's faithfulness gives us courage to continue praying in all circumstances.**
- Read the verses a second time. Invite participants to ponder what they most want to learn or discover about prayer in this small-group experience and to express this desire inwardly to God. Allow a minute of silence.
- Gather the unspoken prayer with words like this:
  O God, you are always with us in love and grace beyond our imagining. Through Christ you call us to come closer to your heart. Through the Spirit you are willing to show us how. Thank you for loving us so deeply and for your faithful guidance. Open our minds and hearts to what you have in store for us in these coming weeks. In Jesus' name. Amen.

- Sing a song or hymn together. Suggestions:

    Traditional: "Near to the Heart of God" (UMH #472)

    Taizé: "O Lord, Hear My Prayer" (TFWS #2200, URWB #390)

PRESENT THE RESOURCES AND GROUP PROCESS *(10 minutes)*

Go over the Introduction in the Participant's Book with group members so that each person understands the process of reading, daily exercises, and journaling, as well as the outline for each group meeting. Here are some items you will want to mention:

Basic flow of the week. Each participant reads the article for the week on Day 1 (the day after the group meeting) and works through the five daily exercises over Days 2 through 6. The group meets on Day 7. Encourage participants' faithfulness to the process. In preparation for the group meeting, suggest that after Exercise 5 they read over their notebook or journal entries for that week.

Basic flow of a group meeting. Explain the various components: Opening, Sharing Insights, Deeper Explorations, and Closing. Summarize for the group the explanatory material found in "A General Outline for Group Meetings" on pages 14–16 of the Introduction in this Leader's Guide.

Materials for each meeting. Ask the members to bring their Bibles, Participant's Books, and journals to each meeting. Because use of the Bible is part of the daily exercises, encourage participants to use a favorite modern translation.

EXPLAIN PARTICIPANT RESPONSIBILITIES *(15 minutes)*

Emphasize the importance of each member's commitment to the daily exercises and practices in making the group process work. If some members have not experienced this type of daily reflection or group interaction, they may need help in feeling comfortable with them. Remind participants: **One of the ways we listen to God is by putting our experiences into words. Throughout the week, we record these experiences in our journal. In the group meeting, we share what we choose to from what we have recorded. Both processes offer clarity and new perspective.**

Present the process of journaling.

Note that some participants may already have experience in the practice of journaling. Call the group's attention to pertinent points from the material on pages 9–11 of the Participant's Book about the value of recording reflections in a journal or personal notebook. Assure them that the writing can be as informal and unstructured as they want. Because each person keeps notes that are most helpful for him or her, the journal becomes a personal record of the spiritual growth this resource encourages.

Consider the commitment of listening.

Group members also commit to listen to and value the words of others:

> As companions together, we give full attention to what God is doing in the life of the one speaking. We learn to listen with our heart as well as our head and to create an accepting space in which all can freely explore their spiritual journeys.

The group becomes a place for deep listening and trusting in God's guiding presence. Let the participants know that developing listening skills is crucial to spiritual formation and that later in the meeting all will have an opportunity to experience a practice called "Holy Listening."

DISCUSS COMMON GROUND RULES *(15 minutes)*

Ground rules are explained fully on page 13 in the Introduction to this Leader's Guide. The rules suggested there will prove helpful but be prepared to offer other possible rules appropriate to the group. You will also want to allow members to make suggestions. Write the completed list on newsprint for the group to see. Remember that the goal is not a formal agreement or covenant but recognition of the basic rules essential for the group to deepen its faith and to mature as a community.

COMPLETE THE PRAYER CARD *(5 minutes)*

The Upper Room Living Prayer Center and its network of prayer volunteers will begin to hold your group in prayer. Simply fill in and mail the card titled "Prayers for Our *Way of Prayer* Group" that is bound into this Guide. Complete the leader's portion of the card by providing your name and your church's mailing address. Please do not use a post office box number. Ask each member of the group to sign his or her first name as evidence of the group's desire to be connected to the larger network of persons involved in *Companions in Christ*.

Break (10 minutes)

Deeper Explorations (35 minutes)

Introduce the "Holy Listening Exercise." (5 minutes)

- This exercise will give everyone a chance to practice prayerful or holy listening, the heart of spiritual friendship and an important element in formational experiences such as the Companions in Christ series. Listening practice is essential to all formational settings: formal or informal, one-on-one, or in a group.

- Give everyone the "Holy Listening Exercise" and "Review Questions" handouts. Explain the process to the group, responding to any questions.

- Ask the group members to pair up for the exercise. As leader you can pair with someone if necessary (you will need to keep track of time, however), or you may assign an unpaired person to be a prayerful listener to a pair.

- Assure participants that each person in the pair will have opportunity to be both a listener and a speaker. After the first eight minutes, they will take two minutes to reflect on the review questions. Then they will trade roles. At the end of the second eight-minute session, they again take two minutes to reflect quietly with the review questions. During the last five minutes they will compare their responses to those questions.

Practice holy listening in pairs. (25 minutes)

- Ask pairs to find a space apart quickly in order to make the most of the time.

- Help participants honor the time by ringing a bell or calling out the time after each eight-minute period and by reminding them to take two minutes to reflect on the review questions. Alert the participants at the close of the two minutes of reflection time to change roles.

- After the second listening session and evaluation, encourage each pair to compare notes on the experience for five minutes.

Gather as a group. (5 minutes)

- Call pairs back into the group to share what they have learned about holy listening.

- Close with this affirmation of the exercise: **There is no greater gift one person can give to another than to listen intently.**

CLOSING (**10 minutes**)

Invite the group to a time of quiet reflection. **What are your hopes for the time ahead of us as companions in Christ? . . . What are your anxieties about these next weeks together? . . . Commit both your hopes and fears to God now in silent prayer. . . .**

Offer a brief word of prayer, asking that all might be able to release their hopes and concerns into God's gracious hands. End with thanksgiving for each person and for God's good purposes in bringing this group together.

Close with song. Choose a favorite hymn.

Remind the members of their weekly assignment to read the article for Week 1 and work through one exercise each day after, recording their thoughts in their journal. Be sure all participants know the location and time of the next meeting and any special responsibilities (such as providing snacks or helping to arrange the worship table).

Holy Listening Exercise

"Spiritual direction takes place when two people agree to give their full attention to what God is doing in one (or both) of their lives and seek to respond in faith."[1]

The purpose of this exercise is for participants to practice holy listening in pairs.

AS THE SPEAKER

Receive your chance to speak and be heard as an opportunity to explore an aspect of your faith experience with which you've struggled a bit during the past week (or day). Remember that you and your friend meet in the company of God, who is the true guiding presence of this time together.

AS THE LISTENER

Practice listening with your heart as well as your head. Create a welcoming, accepting space in which the other person may explore freely his or her journey in your presence and in the presence of God. Be natural, but be alert to any habits or anxious needs in you to analyze, judge, counsel, "fix," teach, or share your own experience. Try to limit your speech to gentle questions and honest words of encouragement.

Be inwardly prayerful as you listen, paying attention to the Spirit even as you listen to the holy mystery of the person before you.

When appropriate and un-intrusive, you might ask the other person to explore simple questions such as these:

- Where did you experience God's grace or presence in the midst of this time?
- Do you sense God calling you to take a step forward in faith or love? Is there an invitation here to explore?

HOW TO BEGIN AND END THE CONVERSATION

- Decide who will be the first listener, and begin with a moment of silent prayer.
- Converse for eight minutes; then pause for two minutes so that each person may respond in silence to the "Review Questions" handout.
- Trade roles and converse for eight minutes more; then pause again for personal review.
- Use the last five minutes to compare notes on your experiences and your responses to the review questions.

Review Questions

FOR THE LISTENER

a. When were you most aware of God's presence (in you, in the other person, between you) in the midst of the conversation?

b. What interrupted or diminished the quality of your presence to God or to the other person?

c. What was the greatest challenge of this experience for you?

FOR THE SPEAKER

a. What was the gift of the conversation for you?

b. What in the listener's manner helped or hindered your ability to pay attention to your life experience and God's presence in it?

c. When were you most aware of God's presence (in you, in the other person, or between you) in the midst of the conversation?

Week 1

How Do You Pray?

PREPARATION

Prepare yourself spiritually. If you are new to leading a formational small group, review once more the Introduction to this Leader's Guide, giving special attention to The Role of the Small-Group Leader and Expectations for the Opening and Sharing Insights Sections of Meetings. Pray for each of your group's participants by name. Ask God's guidance for you as you lead and for your newly forming group as together you embark on this journey into prayer. Read the article for Week 1 and complete the daily exercises, recording your insights in your journal.

Prepare materials and the meeting space.

- As you prepare for each group meeting, refer to Weekly Needs at a Glance, which begins on page 17 of this guide. Review the items listed under All Meetings, as well as the items listed under Week 1, "How Do You Pray?"
- Consider how you will arrange your meeting space for comfort and practicality.
- You will need a Christ candle or other candle to serve as a focal point for your worship table.
- If you wish to introduce the Candle Prayer, preprint it on newsprint and post it in the meeting room.
- Display the ground rules agreed to during the Preparatory Meeting.
- As you complete your daily reflections, pay special attention to Exercise 1, which will provide key background for the Deeper Explorations.
- Review the Weekly Meeting so you are thoroughly familiar with it and can lead without reading everything from the book.
- Select songs to sing or recorded music to play for the Opening and Closing.

- Look ahead to the Week 4 "Deeper Explorations" process. If you can see from your group size that you will need more time for "Sharing Musical Prayer," you will need to negotiate the time frame for that meeting with your group at the end of this week's meeting (see page 35).

Review the intent of this meeting: That participants will become more aware of their personal histories with prayer and find freedom to think broadly together about what prayer is.

OPENING (10 MINUTES)

Welcome all participants by name as they enter.

Set a context.

> **Welcome to *The Way of Prayer*! Over the next ten weeks we will explore a variety of ways to pray, some or many of which may be new to you. As we begin this journey into a richer and more satisfying prayer life, we want to review our own personal histories with prayer— how we've been taught to think of and to practice it. Then we can begin to expand our perspectives and practices.**

Join together in worship.

- Light the candle at the center of the group. As you light it, ask participants to join you in reciting the Candle Prayer; or welcome Christ's presence with words such as these: **The light of this candle reminds us that Christ, our living teacher, is present with us now as we gather to begin this new venture into a deeper life of prayer.**

- Read Psalm 84:1-4 aloud at an unhurried pace.

- Invite participants to ponder: What does your soul long for? What makes your heart and your flesh sing for joy to God?

- Read the passage again, leaving a minute for reflection.

- Invite members to share briefly how this passage spoke to their hearts.

- Offer a simple prayer of thanks and praise.

- *Sing a song.* Suggestions:

    Traditional: "Joyful, Joyful, We Adore Thee" (UMH #89, URWB #65)

    Contemporary: "How Lovely, Lord, How Lovely" (TFWS #2042)

SHARING INSIGHTS (45 MINUTES)

In this part of the meeting, group members will identify and share where they have experienced God's presence in their lives this past week, as related to the week's article and daily exercises. Begin by reminding group members of the theme for this week—that there are many and various ways to pray.

1. Give participants time to review briefly the article for this week and their journal entries for the daily exercises, noting parts of the article or daily exercises that they found especially meaningful. *(5 minutes)*

2. Ask group members to share insights from the weekly reading and their journal entries. As leader, model the sharing by offering your brief reflections first. Encourage deep and active listening. If the group numbers more than eight, you may want to form two groups to ensure that everyone can participate in the sharing. *(35 minutes)*

3. Conclude by asking the group to identify any common themes they heard in this sharing time. *(5 minutes)*

BREAK (10 MINUTES)

DEEPER EXPLORATIONS (45 MINUTES)

Encourage exploration of past and present experiences with prayer.

Introduce the theme. (1 minute)

> We've all learned something about prayer over the course of our lives. Some of us have learned particular ways to pray in our families or churches. We may have picked up ideas from friends, reading, or simply experimenting. Exercise 1 gave you a chance to reflect on your own experience with prayer in relation to scriptural models. We're going to take a little more time now to review our personal histories with prayer, beginning with individual reflection. You might want to review your response to Exercise 1, then see how responding to these reflection questions takes you further.

Spend time with the reflection sheet. (10 minutes)

Give each participant a copy of the reflection sheet "My Personal History with Prayer" on page 36 to complete.

Share in pairs. (9 minutes)

Invite each person to pair with one other person and tell the other what each feels comfortable telling from his or her personal history with prayer.

Regather group to explore what renews us spiritually. (25 minutes total)

- Take five minutes to journal, asking yourself, "What activities truly renew my spirit?" Name in writing what you can recall having done over the years that has deepened your awareness of God or strengthened your relationship with Christ. For example: worship, absorbing the wonder of creation, conversation with a spiritual friend, devotional reading, acts of service or hospitality.

- *Share responses in group. (5 minutes)*

- *Invite people to go further, thinking beyond the expected. (10 minutes)*
  — What activities reenergize you, even if they seem nonreligious?
  — What kinds of things help you feel connected to a deeper universal reality, a sense of common relationship with all people/creatures?

- *Share responses out loud and let ideas build within group. (5 minutes)*
  Ask if they can see these activities as prayer. Why or why not? What is prayer?

CLOSING *(10 minutes)*

- *Read Psalm 42:1-3 aloud.* Invite the participants to focus silently on their yearning for God. Ask them to ponder: **What does your yearning feel like inside? Does it have a shape, color, texture, or weight?**

- *Ask participants how they would express their yearning in words.* Allow them to speak.

- *Now ask them to close their eyes and express their yearning in gestures or a posture.* After several moments, invite people to hold their posture/gesture, open their eyes, and quietly take in with appreciation how each person expresses his or her yearning.

- *Option:* If your group members are well acquainted with one another and feel comfortable with spontaneity, suggest they form a group tableau that expresses their common yearning to know God more deeply in prayer.

- *Invite all to join hands in a circle.* Quote this statement from Father Edward Farrell: "**Prayer is a hunger, a hunger that is not easily quieted.**"[1] Offer a prayer of gratitude for how God has made us eternally hungry for relationship with God and for all the ways the Spirit draws us closer to the divine heart.

- *Sing a song and offer a closing benediction.* Song suggestions:
  Traditional: "Prayer Is the Soul's Sincere Desire" (UMH #492)
  Contemporary: "To Know You More" (TFWS #2161)

- *Extinguish the candle.* As you do, remind all present to carry the light of Christ within them through this week's journey.

- *Remind the group of the time and location of the next meeting.* If you will need a longer time for the Week 4 meeting due to number in the group, be sure to negotiate this with your group now.

My Personal History with Prayer

- As a child, what did you learn or discover about prayer (through instruction, observation, experience)? From whom did you primarily learn?

- What specific ways were you taught to pray (traditional prayers, methods, gestures/postures)? List or sketch them.

- How was silence a positive or negative experience for you growing up?

- When do you recall first having a desire to come closer to God?

Week 2
Images of God

PREPARATION

Prepare yourself spiritually. Read the article for Week 2; reflect on all the daily exercises, and write in your journal. Pray for your ability as a leader to be open to the guiding presence of God's Spirit through the meeting. Pray also for each participant and for your group as a whole for openness to seeing new images and hearing fresh names for God.

Prepare materials and the meeting space.

- Refer to Weekly Needs at a Glance on page 17 of this guide. Review the items listed under All Meetings as well as under this week's title, "Images of God."

- Consider how you will arrange the meeting space for comfort and practicality.

- Arrange chairs in a circle or around a table.

- Include a Christ candle or other candle to serve as a focal point for worship.

- If you use the Candle Prayer, post it alongside the group ground rules in a visible place.

- On one sheet of newsprint list in advance divine names/images from scripture (see Daily Exercises 2 and 3). On a second sheet, list divine names/images found in hymns and songs (see suggested sources on page 42; if you do not have access to *The Faith We Sing* for your group, you may wish to secure a copy for yourself in order to draw on the song "Bring Many Names," #2047).

- Drawing from the two newsprint lists, create a list of divine names for the Closing on a piece of paper. For groups of eight to twelve, select one name per person. For smaller groups ou may list up to two names per person.

- Select songs to sing or recorded music to play for the Opening and Closing.

Review the intent of this meeting: To explore those images of God that might stretch us and to discover how names for God and images of God connect in our prayer life.

OPENING (10 MINUTES)

Welcome all participants as they enter.

Set a context.

> In this second weekly meeting, we will explore more fully our response to a variety of names and images for God. We will look especially at the relationship between our current images of God and the way we actually pray.

Join together in worship.

- Light the candle in the midst of your worship setting. Bid the group join you in saying the Candle Prayer, or offer words such as these: **May the brightness of this candle remind us that only the light of Christ can illumine the depths of our hearts, guiding us into the fullness of God's truth. Amen.**

- Read this quote from author Calvin Miller: **"Your friendship with God is rooted in a paradox. You reach to God as you seek to maintain a critical balance—the balance between intimacy and awe."**[1]

- Ask participants to ponder silently how they balance intimacy and awe in their relationship with God. Does their prayer life tend more toward one or the other? Allow a moment for quiet reflection.

- Read Ephesians 1:3-6, 13-14 without rushing. Point out that this passage speaks of each Person of the Trinity. Invite participants to think about each Person of the Trinity. Do they relate to each one primarily in terms of awe or intimacy? Allow a minute for reflection.

- Read the passage again, and invite the group to let the words lead them into a time of silent prayer. Allow two minutes of silence, then close with a brief prayer of thanks for the loving mystery of God's presence to us in and through each Person of the Holy Trinity.

- Close with a song. Suggestions:
    Traditional: "Maker, in Whom We Live" (UMH #88)
    Contemporary: "Glorify Thy Name" (TFWS #2016)

SHARING INSIGHTS (45 MINUTES)

During the next forty-five minutes, participants will identify and speak of the ways they have experienced God's presence this week. Key to this sharing are the insights and experiences participants had while reading the week's article and doing the daily exercises. Begin by reminding group members of this week's theme—exploring images and names for God in relation to our prayer.

1. Ask participants to review briefly this week's article and their journal entries in response to the daily exercises. *(5 minutes)*

2. Invite participants to share insights from the article and their journal entries. Offer your own brief reflections first. Encourage the group to practice deep and active listening during this time. *(35 minutes)*

3. Take a few moments to identify common themes that have emerged from your mutual exchange. What themes especially spoke to or touched the group? Where did God seem most present? *(5 minutes)*

BREAK *(10 minutes)*

Post the two newsprint sheets with the divine names and images from scriptural sources and from select hymns (See Leader's Note, page 42).

DEEPER EXPLORATIONS (45 MINUTES)

Consider together how images of God affect our actual prayer life.

Set a context. (1 minute)

> We have been exploring various names and images of God all week. We want to look now at how our images of God have changed over time, how our names and images for God affect each other, and how they actually guide our prayer in actual life circumstances. We will also pray with an image or name for God that may stretch us a bit beyond our comfort zone.

Group reviews divine names/images. (9 minutes)

- Review the divine names/images from scriptural sources posted on newsprint (from Daily Exercises 2 and 3); add others participants may have discovered or been influenced by.

- Review the divine names/images from select hymns as listed on newsprint. Which seem fresh or surprising?

- Consider to what extent common worship is the source of divine names/images that either constrict or expand our personal language of prayer.

- Discuss which images seem less familiar or more challenging to pray with.

Personal reflection with journal (15 minutes)

- Ask participants to spend five minutes pondering and writing in their journals about how their images of God have changed or expanded over the course of their lives. What has most shaped or reshaped their thinking?

- Invite them to choose one of the less familiar, more challenging images of God and spend ten minutes praying with it to see where it takes them. Give a gentle verbal signal or sound a quiet chime tone to end this prayer time.

Share responses in regathered group (20 minutes)

- Invite participants to share from their personal reflection time: first, about how their images of God have changed over time; then, noting what it was like to pray with a less familiar image of God.

- As sharing continues, look for opportunities to ask probing questions such as these:

    1. **How do you ordinarily address God in prayer? How have changes in your image of God shifted your way of naming God in prayer? What is the relationship between our images of God and our ways of naming God in prayer?** (For example, one's image of God may slowly shift to a less masculine one; yet out of habit one continues simply to address God as "Lord." Or the adjectives used to describe God may shift, for example, from "Almighty God" to "Gracious God.")

    2. **What images of God predominate in your personal prayer at times of crisis, such as when you become seriously ill, a loved one dies prematurely, or a national trauma occurs?** Note that our most deeply rooted ideas about God surface at times like these. Ideas about God can change in our minds sooner than they shift in our hearts. You will want to encourage patience and openness to God's timing in these matters.

CLOSING (10 MINUTES)

- *Invite a time of silent reflection on today's group meeting experience.*

- *Explain the process for closing prayers:* As leader you have selected a number of names/images for God. You will address God with a particular name, then the person to your right will offer a brief phrase of praise or petition in relation to the divine name. Moving around the circle, each person will complete a prayer until you have spoken all the names for God (in smaller groups, members may complete more than one prayer). Give an example of the process:

— Leader: O Good Shepherd of the sheep, . . . (person next to leader completes prayer with phrase relating to image such as: Feed us in your green pastures)

— Leader: Holy Comforter and Advocate, . . . (next person completes prayer, such as: Stand by us and assure us of your grace), and so on around the circle.

After your explanation, take time to become quiet and prayerful again. Assure everyone there is no need to rush. Invite participants to let their prayer phrase emerge from deep within their hearts as they savor the name and image of God you speak.

• *Pray together in this way.*

• *Invite participants to carry home a chosen name for God with their own prayer phrase.*

• *Alert them to the importance of completing the daily exercises,* especially Exercises 3 and 5, which will be the basis for Sharing Insights time next week.

• *Sing a song and offer a benediction.* Song suggestions:

Traditional: "Source and Sovereign, Rock and Cloud" (UMH #113) or "The God of Abraham Praise" (UMH #116)

Contemporary: "Bring Many Names" (TFWS #2047) or "Mothering God, You Gave Me Birth" (TFWS #2050)

Leader's Note

IMAGES AND NAMES FOR GOD FROM HYMNS AND SONGS

Look up the following hymns and songs if you have access to *The United Methodist Hymnal* or *The Faith We Sing*. Otherwise, peruse your own hymnals and songbooks to glean as much variation in names for and images of God as you can find. List these in advance on newsprint for the Deeper Explorations time.

"The God of Abraham Praise" (UMH #116)

"Source and Sovereign, Rock and Cloud" (UMH #113)

"Bring Many Names" (TFWS #2047)

"Womb of Life" (TFWS #2046)

"God the Sculptor of the Mountains" (TFWS #2060)

Week 3
Praying by Heart

PREPARATION

Prepare yourself spiritually. Read the article for Week 3; reflect on each daily exercise, and write in your journal. Pray for the renewing breath of God to fill you so that your guidance of the group meeting will be Spirit-led. Pray for the same Spirit of new life to touch each participant according toneed and to prepare all for your group meeting. In reviewing the Leader's Guide for this week's meeting, pay special attention to the Leader's Note on pages 47–48.

Prepare materials and the meeting space.

- Refer to Weekly Needs at a Glance in the opening pages of this guide, briefly reviewing the items listed under All Meetings and checking items indicated for this week's title, "Praying by Heart."
- Arrange chairs in a circle or around a table, with a cloth and the Christ candle as a worship focal point. You may wish to add your chime or bell to the worship center.
- If desired, have the Candle Prayer and ground rules posted in a visible place in the room.
- Select songs from songbooks or play recorded music for the Opening and Closing.

Review the intent of this meeting: To discover the gift of praying heart or breath prayers together with others and for the sake of others.

OPENING *(10 minutes)*

Welcome all participants as they enter.

Set a context.

> This week we will start by sharing our personal experience with prayers of the heart and breath prayers. Then we'll expand our practice from the personal to the corporate. How might we pray our heart and breath prayers both together and for others?

Join together in worship.

- Light the candle and ask your group to join you in praying the Candle Prayer or offer words such as these: **We light this candle as a reminder of Christ's presence with us and of the renewing action of the Holy Spirit breathing within and among us. We are on holy ground! Amen.**

- Read the following quote from Thomas Kelly's beloved modern classic, *A Testament of Devotion*: **"There is a way of life so hid with Christ in God that in the midst of the day's business one is inwardly lifting brief prayers, short [bursts] of praise, subdued whispers of adoration and of tender love to the Beyond that is within."**[1]

- Ask participants to reflect quietly on these words in relation to their daily prayer exercises this past week. Did they experience something of the truth Kelly describes? After a pause, invite brief responses.

- Read Romans 8:26: **"Likewise the Spirit helps us in our weakness; for we do not know how to pray as we ought, but that very Spirit intercedes with sighs too deep for words."**

- Invite brief sentence prayers of thanks and praise from the group. Gather these prayers with your own closing words. If you wish, invite a musical response after each prayer, such as the Byzantine chant "Let Us Pray to the Lord" (UMH #485), which incorporates echoes of the ancient Jesus Prayer.

- Close with a song or hymn. Suggestions:

    Traditional: "Let It Breathe on Me" (UMH #503)

    Contemporary: "Lord, Listen to Your Children Praying" (TFWS #2193)

SHARING INSIGHTS (45 MINUTES)

Encourage group members to name ways in which they have experienced God's presence and guidance this past week, especially in relation to the week's reading and daily exercises. Remind them of the theme—praying in the tradition of the Jesus Prayer and in personalized forms of the ancient prayer of the heart.

1. Let participants briefly review the article and their journal entries for this week, giving special attention to Exercises 3 and 5. *(5 minutes)*

2. Invite them to contribute their insights. Give all a chance to share the process of discovering a personal Jesus Prayer or breath prayer. Ask them to consider what prayer has stayed with them. Invite reflection on how they experienced using heart or breath rhythms to help carry their prayer. As leader, model the sharing by offering your own brief thoughts first. Encourage deep and active listening. *(35 minutes)*

3. Point out any common themes or refrains that you heard during the discussion. Ask, **What might the Spirit be saying to us through these themes?** *(5 minutes)*

BREAK (10 MINUTES)

DEEPER EXPLORATIONS (45 MINUTES)

Learn to pray one another's breath prayers in various situations.

Introduce the theme. (1 minute)

> The breath prayer is a way of personalizing the ancient prayer of the heart, or Jesus Prayer. We have been experimenting with various forms of unceasing prayer, using heart and breath rhythms as an aid. Now we want to explore what can happen when we pray one another's breath prayers together, both in our group time and beyond it.

Sharing breath prayers in pairs (14 minutes)

- Invite everyone to find a partner. (Note: If your group has an odd number you may pair with someone but will still need to track timing for group. You can experience the shared prayer for several minutes and quietly check your watch once or twice.)

- Encourage each pair to find a quiet space to sit together and listen carefully to each other's prayers and breath rhythms.

- One person shares with the other his or her personal Jesus Prayer or breath prayer, including a little background to the prayer (if comfortable doing so) and how the words move in rhythm with the breath.

- Partners silently pray that person's prayer together for about four minutes, allowing their breathing rhythms gradually to coordinate if possible. If partners cannot hear or sense each other's breathing rhythm, they might gently place their hands on the other's back to feel the rhythm until they sense being in sync. Encourage pairs to let the prayer carry them into God's presence together. (As leader, ring bell or chime five minutes after pairs begin.)

- After the chime sounds, the other person shares his or her personal prayer and the pair repeats the process.

- After the second chime, pairs share what it was like to pray together this way. (If you have paired with someone, be sure to track these last five minutes of time as well.)

Sharing in regathered group (10 minutes)

Ask how the pairs experienced praying each other's prayers and what it was like to share a breathing rhythm. Invite expression of feelings, insights, and impressions.

Discussing ways to make breath prayers a wider ministry (20 minutes)

- Talk about sharing breath prayers in various settings, giving illustrations (see Leader's Note on pages 47–48):

  — Praying with children and other family members at home

  — Praying with the ill in hospital or nursing home settings

  — Praying with a spiritual friend/mentee/prayer partner

- Encourage participants to think for five minutes about when and where they might share such prayers in their own particular life situations, jotting down ideas in their journals.

- Invite participants to share their ideas, as they are comfortable.

- Encourage sharing this way of prayer with family and friends in the coming weeks.

Closing (10 minutes)

- Read these words from Dietrich Bonhoeffer: "**Who prays the Psalms? David (Solomon, Asaph, etc.) prays, Christ prays, we pray. We—that is, first of all the entire community in which alone the vast richness of the Psalter can be prayed, but also finally every individual insofar as he participates in Christ and his community and prays their prayer.**"[2]

- Invite participants to spend five minutes in silence praying their breath prayers as prayers of intercession for others in the world who share the same deeply felt need or desire as they do. They might ask God to reveal others who need their prayer.

- Invite brief sharing of how people experienced praying their personal breath prayer as an act of intercession.

- Sing a song of praise or offer a prayer of thanksgiving. Song suggestions:

    Spiritual: "Kum Ba Yah" (UMH #494)

    Taize: "Come and Fill Our Hearts" (TFWS #2157; URWB, #378)

- Announce: **Be sure to complete Exercise 2 this week, and bring with you to our next meeting an audiotape or CD of music that expresses prayer for you. Your sharing will be the content of our Deeper Explorations next week.** Remind group of added time commitment next week if this applies

- Offer a benediction.

Leader's Note

Although the breath prayer is individualized and personal,
it can also be shared.[3]

—Ron DelBene

Breath prayer can be helpful in many settings with other people in your life. In his book *Into the Light*, author Ron DelBene describes how breath prayer can be shared when people face serious illness, long-term limitations, or end of life. Ron suggests introducing the breath prayer in a casual way in the course of ordinary conversation when the moment seems ripe: "There's something a lot of people have found helpful in times of illness (or loneliness or waiting), and you might find it helpful too. It's called the breath prayer." If the person shows interest, you can help him or her find a breath prayer with a few simple questions:

1. When you pray, what do you usually call God? (Lord, Jesus, God, Spirit, Creator, Father, Holy One)

2. If Jesus (or God) were standing before you right now, asking, "(Name), what do you want?" how would you respond?

Help people find a simple phrase that puts together their name for God and their request in a way that is comfortable to speak and remember. Write the prayer phrase out on two index cards (one for the other person and one for you). Invite the people to become familiar with the prayer, allowing it to become a daily companion. Help them think of ways to prompt themselves to remember to pray their breath prayer frequently through the day (taping the card to a mirror, putting it in a place they will see often). Offer to pray their prayer with them as often as you can remember, or at specific times of day when you give yourself to intercessory prayer. You may suggest that this prayer be shared with other family members (spouses, children, siblings, parents, extended family), friends, church members, caregivers, or medical personnel.

Under more ordinary circumstances, breath prayer can also be a valuable way to share prayer. For example, when each person in a family discovers his or her own breath prayer, family members can then pray for each other by praying each member's breath prayer *with* them (aloud together or in spirit when apart). You might choose particular days of each week to focus on one family member's breath prayer.

Family members can also request special remembrance of their prayers on days when they face particular challenges, needs, or stresses.

Another possibility is to share breath prayers with a spiritual friend, prayer partner, or spiritual mentor. It is a simple way to stay united in prayer when you are not physically together.

Many graces can be given when we pray in such ways with others. Breath prayer helps us to stay attuned to God's presence each day. Thus we can anticipate receiving new insight, assurance, and conviction from the Spirit in God's good time. Stay alert with humble expectation and hope!

Week 4
Praying with Music

PREPARATION

Prepare yourself spiritually. Read the article for Week 4; reflect on each of the daily exercises, and record your responses in your journal. Pray for the grace to be a clear, gentle, and joyful leader within the group. Pray also that each participant might experience the depth of grace and power in musical prayer this week.

Prepare materials and the meeting space.

- Refer to Weekly Needs at a Glance, briefly reviewing items listed under All Meetings, as well as this week's title, "Praying with Music."

- Be sure to select a CD or audiocassette tape of music from Exercise 2 to share with the group. You may send a brief reminder to participants (via e-mail, telephone, or postcard) to complete this exercise and bring a piece of music to play for the group meeting.

- You also need to select an instrumental or vocal selection to play for the Opening. Choose music that will help members become collected and quiet as you begin.

- It is especially important to bring song into this session. If group members are reluctant to sing, bring recorded accompaniment they can sing along with for Opening and Closing worship times.

- Be sure to locate a CD or audiocassette player with good sound quality.

- Estimate the approximate time needed for all participants to play the piece they bring.

- If you use newsprint for the Closing, bring masking tape since you will likely need at least two sheets of paper visible to the group, one with the musical refrains and one with the acrostic. If you have use of a chalkboard or whiteboard, there should be room to list these two parts side by side.

- Arrange chairs in a circle or around a table with the cloth and Christ candle in the center. You might add symbols of music to the worship center or invite participants to place their CDs or audiocassettes around the candle when they arrive for the meeting.
- If desired, have the Candle Prayer and ground rules posted for all to see.

Review the intent of the meeting: To share with one another how music is a vessel of prayer, individually and in community.

OPENING (10 MINUTES)

Welcome all participants as they enter.

Set a context.

> **Welcome to Week 4 of our exploration into ways of understanding and practicing prayer. This week our focus has been on music as an avenue into prayer and a vital expression of prayer. In our meeting we will have opportunities to describe what we have discovered over the week and to tell how music becomes prayer for us.**

Join together in worship.

- Enter a spirit of worship by lighting the candle on the table. Recite together the Candle Prayer, or offer words such as these: **The light of Christ shines among us, revealing God's beauty and truth in more ways than we can imagine. Thanks be to God! Amen.**
- Invite participants to take a few deep breaths, quiet their minds, and still their bodies as they listen to the music selection you have chosen for this opening worship. Ask them to enter this time as prayer, allowing the music to carry them into God's loving presence.
- Play the instrumental or song selection you have chosen.
- Read Psalm 92:1-4 without rushing.
- Sing a song or hymn together. Suggestions:
    Traditional: "When in Our Music God Is Glorified" (UMH #68)
    Spiritual: "I'm Goin' a Sing When the Spirit Says Sing" (UMH #333)
    Contemporary: "I Sing Praises to Your Name" (TFWS #2037)

SHARING INSIGHTS (45 MINUTES)

Encourage group members to name ways in which they have experienced God's presence this past week, especially in relation to the reading and daily exercises. Remind them of the theme—rediscovering the spiritual power of music and learning to pray through it.

1. Let participants review the article and their journal entries for this week. *(5 minutes)*

2. Invite them to contribute their insights, saving responses to Exercise 2 for the Deeper Explorations. As leader, model the sharing by offering your own brief reflections first. Encourage deep and active listening to one another and to God. *(35 minutes)*

3. Invite participants to identify common themes or refrains they may have heard during the discussion. Ask, **What might the Spirit be singing to us through these common themes?** *(5 minutes)*

BREAK (10 MINUTES)

DEEPER EXPLORATIONS (45 MINUTES)

Share together various experiences of music as prayer.

Introduce the theme. (2 minutes)

This week we have been exploring various forms of musical prayer. The psalmist tells us to "make a joyful noise to the LORD" (100:1). Over the next forty minutes we will share with one another a particular musical expression that is, for us, a "joyful noise" to our Maker. You were asked last week to complete Exercise 2 and to bring an audiocassette or CD of music to this meeting with a selection that expresses something of your own spirit in prayer. Hopefully, each of us has a song or other piece of music to share.

Share musical prayer. (40 minutes)

- Invite each person in turn to share the selection of music he or she has brought. Designate a time limit for each person, depending on the number in your group. For example, if your group numbers eight persons, ask that each selection be played for no more than three minutes (leaving about two minutes each for the presenter to speak about the music and to hear feedback from others in the group as described below).

- After each piece, ask the presenter to describe what makes this music an experience of prayer. You might prompt responses with a few questions: **What of your soul or spirit does it express? What kind of prayer is it? Does it shift you from one mood or posture of prayer to another?**

- If time allows, invite brief responses from others in the group. What does this music evoke in them? If the presenter has difficulty articulating how the music expresses prayer or leads to prayer, invite responses from the group.

Summarize your experience. (3 minutes)

Ask, **What is it like to hear one another's musical prayers and how each person experiences them as prayer?**

CLOSING (10 MINUTES)

- Name two common themes from Sharing Insights or Deeper Explorations.
- Reduce each theme to a single word and list theme words on newsprint, chalkboard, or whiteboard. Think of a few well-known hymn or chant stanzas that could express these themes in a short musical refrain. List stanzas after each word. For example:
  — Spirit: "Spirit of the living God, fall afresh on me" (sung as last phrase of song)
  — Heart: "Heart of my own heart, whatever befall, still be my vision, O Ruler of all" (from "Be Thou My Vision")

  Then select one word and musical stanza you feel would work well for the process described below. Mark it with an asterisk.
- Form an acrostic with the theme word. List its letters vertically. Then invite participants in turn, or the whole group together, to create a sentence describing or expanding on the theme, starting with each letter of the acrostic. Write these on newsprint or chalkboard. For example:

  H: How lovely is God's music at the heart of creation!
  E: Every creature sings in its own unique voice.
  A: All people, come sing God's praises from your heart!
  R: Reach deep into your soul and find the music there.
  T: Teach your lips to sing the vision in your soul.

- "Sing" your new song. Have a person read each line of the acrostic, followed with the selected musical stanza sung by all together. Go around your circle until all the lines of the acrostic have been read, each followed by the sung refrain.*
- Offer a brief prayer of thanks for the gift of music and for the joy of your common song.
- Announce: **Be sure to complete Exercises 3 and 4 this week; be ready to bring with you next week the photos or pictures described in these exercises.**
- Offer a benediction.

---

* **Option:** You may prefer a simpler closing process. After identifying common themes from this weekly meeting, invite the group to find or think of songs that connect with these themes. Select a few to sing from your hymnals/songbooks. Allow a time of silence for everyone to absorb the sound and meaning of these songs. Then continue the Closing from the prayer of thanks onward.

Week 5
Praying by Gaze

PREPARATION

Prepare yourself spiritually. Read the article for Week 5; reflect on each daily exercise, and record responses in your journal. Pray for your physical eyes and the eyes of your heart to be open to what God wants to reveal this week. Pray likewise for each participant's eyes to be opened so that the Spirit may bring needed gifts of insight to the group meeting.

Prepare materials and the meeting space.

- Review the Weekly Needs at a Glance for items listed under All Meetings as well as those listed under this week's title, "Praying by Gaze."
- Familiarize yourself with the process of the upcoming weekly meeting.
- Select a large icon of Jesus (8" by 10" or larger) that the group can contemplate together, preferably an icon different from the one in the Participant's Book. If you cannot locate such an icon, find a quality reproduction of a good painting or drawing of Jesus' face.
- Be sure to select a photo of a loved one and a picture of a stranger from your own work with Daily Exercises 3 and 4 to share with the group.
- Set up the room with chairs in a circle and a Christ candle at the center on a cloth-covered table large enough to hold the icon for the Deeper Explorations. Post the Candle Prayer and ground rules if you need them.
- Select songs and songbooks or recorded music to play for the Opening and Closing.

Review the intent of this meeting: To experience praying by gaze together in a variety of ways, and to share with one another how this practice leads us closer to God.

OPENING (10 MINUTES)

Welcome all participants as they enter.

Set a context.

> We have arrived at the midpoint, Week 5, in our ten-week journey through *The Way of Prayer*. The form of prayer we've been exploring this week, praying by gaze, is perhaps one of the most fascinating and least familiar ways of prayer for Western Christians. Yet it may also feel quite natural to us. Today we will continue exploring this pathway of prayer, sharing our questions, experiences, and insights together.

Join together in worship.

- Light the candle and recite together the Candle Prayer, or offer a prayer such as this: **Holy God, we come into your presence now, aware that you are a mystery always beyond our knowing. Yet you choose also to be near us in mercy and loving-kindness. Guide our perceptions as we turn our gaze to you, and open the eyes of our hearts to see what you would reveal to us this day. Amen.**

- Sing quietly one of the following familiar songs: "Open Our Eyes" (TFWS #2086) or verse 1 of "Open My Eyes, That I May See" (UMH #454)

- Invite two to three minutes of silent gazing on the icon of Jesus on the back flap of the Participant's Book cover.

- Bid one-sentence or phrase prayers from the group, expressing what is in their hearts.

- Sing again one of the two songs listed above, or play a quiet piece of music. Then say, **Amen.**

SHARING INSIGHTS (45 MINUTES)

You and your group members will share insights and experiences of God's presence in your lives this past week, especially in relation to the weekly reading and daily exercises. With respect to daily exercises, ask the group to focus during this time on Exercises 1, 2, and 5, leaving Exercises 3 and 4 for the Deeper Explorations time.

1. Ask participants to review the article and their journal entries for this week. *(5 minutes)*

2. Invite them to contribute their insights, saving responses to Exercises 3 and 4 for the Deeper Explorations. As leader, model the sharing by offering your own brief reflections first. Encourage deep and active listening to one another and to God. *(35 minutes)*

3. Invite participants to identify common themes or refrains they have heard during the discussion. Ask, **How is the Spirit speaking to us through these refrains?** *(5 minutes)*

BREAK (10 MINUTES)

DEEPER EXPLORATIONS (45 MINUTES)

Explore praying with icons and other images.

Introduce the theme. (5 minutes)

Our practice of gazing prayer is rooted in the great Christian tradition of praying with icons. Henri J. M. Nouwen writes, "The mystery of the Incarnation is that it has become possible to see God in and through Jesus Christ. Christ is the image of God."[1] We are going to begin our Deeper Explorations by praying with this icon of Jesus—an image of the One who is called "the image of the invisible God" (Col. 1:15). Indicate the icon or picture you have placed in full view of the group. (The group may need to gather on one side of the room so all can see clearly.)

Praying with icons is a form of contemplative prayer. Remember, contemplative prayer is natural to all human beings, not an esoteric practice. Ask participants to listen carefully to these words of Henri Nouwen. Read slowly, with meaning:

> **Contemplative prayer can be described as an imagining of Christ, a letting him enter fully into our consciousness so that he becomes the icon always present in our inner room. By looking at Christ with loving attention, we learn with our minds and hearts what it means that he is the way to [God].[2]**

Pray with the icon of Christ. (10 minutes)

Invite the group members to contemplate the icon of Christ with loving attention for the next ten minutes, imagining him fully, letting the reality of his spirit enter their minds and hearts in the silence.

Reflect on the experience. (5 minutes)

Invite simple reflections on this time of prayer as people feel moved to share.

Guide an exercise in seeing others as "icons." (25 minutes)

- Invite participants to broaden their perspective now, from praying with a classic icon of Jesus to praying with "icons" of other people. Read the following words from Nouwen:

    > **Contemplative prayer is the way we come to know God by heart. When we know [God] by heart, then we will also recognize [God] in our world, its nature, its history, and its people.[3]**

- Invite brief sharing from Exercise 3, the experience of praying with an icon or image of a loved one. Gently prompt responses with questions like these: **Where did your gazing take you? In what ways did you sense the difference between regarding someone from a human versus a spiritual point of view?** *(5 minutes)*

- Now invite brief sharing from Exercise 4, the experience of praying with images of persons who are total strangers or from whom we feel distant due to geographic, cultural, economic, or religious differences. Again, prompt responses with questions: **What about this gazing did you find difficult? Where did your praying by gaze take you?** *(5 minutes)*

- Instruct everyone to put the two pictures side by side and to take a minute to gaze at them together. Then ask, **What is it like to juxtapose a loved one beside someone unknown, distant, or difficult to understand?** Share your perceptions in a single word, phrase, or sentence. *(3 minutes)*

- Quickly create a group collage of the "strangers," taping or pasting their pictures onto a piece of poster board. Ask, **How might we see these persons as the ones Jesus calls "the least of these"? How are we called to pray for them? with them?** *(5 minutes)*

- Have participants hold a loved one's photo at arm's length so they can see the image superimposed on the collage. Invite them to gaze on their loved one in relation to all those strangers behind them in the collage. Remind them that just as they have a particular, personal relationship of love with this one person, so God has a particular, personal relationship with each person in that collage. Invite them to see with the eyes of Christ as they look at all these pictures together. *(3 minutes)*

- Share responses briefly. *(4 minutes)*

CLOSING (10 MINUTES)

- Place the Christ icon on your focus table with a cloth, surrounded by votive candles. Invite others to help you light the candles.

- Place your group collage at the base of the table, and allow group members to place their loved ones' photos either on the table or leaning up against the collage.

- Enter into a time of silent reflection and prayer as you gaze at the gathered images.

- Read the following words from Gunilla Norris, noting that they address God:

   In You nothing and no one is forgotten.
   How vast and providential is the memory
   with which You keep us all.
   It is only we who forget You

and then one another.
It is we who starve each other
and exclude each other.
Give me new eyes.[4]

- Sing a song. Suggestions:

   Traditional: "Open My Eyes, That I May See" (UMH #454, verse 1 only)

   Contemporary: "Open Our Eyes" (TFWS #2086)

   Taizé: "Bless the Lord, My Soul" (sing several times)

- Offer a brief prayer of thanks and a closing benediction.

Week 6
Praying with Our Bodies

PREPARATION

Prepare yourself spiritually. Read the article for Week 6; reflect on the daily exercises, and keep your journal. Pray that you will know a deeper joy in your own embodiment of prayer this week and that participants will discover new ways to honor their bodies as temples of the Spirit.

Prepare materials and the meeting space.

- Refer to Weekly Needs at a Glance to review items listed for all meetings and especially under this week's title, "Praying with Our Bodies." Prepare the four scripture texts found under Deeper Explorations on folded paper or card stock. Have tape/backing ready to post or prop the scripture texts at each station during the break.

- Familiarize yourself with the group process of the weekly meeting.

- Arrange chairs in a circle or around a table, placing the Christ candle as a central focal point. If the group uses the Candle Prayer, post it alongside the ground rules.

- Be sure to allow enough space in each corner of the meeting room for several people to be at each station.

- Select in advance the Lord's Prayer or a psalm/psalm portion (six to eight verses are ideal) for the second part of the Deeper Explorations. Suggestions: Psalm 46, selected verses; Psalm 84:1-4, 10-12; Psalm 95: 1-7; Psalm 100.

- Select songs or recorded music for worship times. Locate a copy of *The Faith We Sing* in order to make use of the song "Sacred the Body" (TFWS #2228). Few songs are so well fitted to this week's theme.

Review the intent of the meeting: To experience more fully praying with our bodies through gesture, posture, and focus on the physical senses as an avenue of grace.

OPENING (10 MINUTES)

Welcome all participants as they enter.

Set a context.

> This week we have been considering the place of our bodies in prayer. To some of us this topic may feel challenging or freeing or both. In our time together now, let's open ourselves in prayer to whatever the Spirit of God would further teach us about the gift of our bodies as vessels and expressers of prayer.

Join together in worship.

- Light the candle and say together the Candle Prayer, or offer words such as these: **Creator God, you have made us in a wonderful and mysterious way, connecting body, mind, and spirit as an integrated whole. Help us to honor your creative gift to us by finding joy and freedom in learning to pray with all of who we are. In the name of Christ, who came in human form to heal us, body and soul. Amen.**

- Read the following passage from Gunilla Norris's book *Being Home*:

  > Sometimes saying prayers keeps us from being prayers. Words come then not in response to life but in substitution for life. We think the map is the territory and we are untouched by the smells and wonders of actual living.[1]

- Suggest reflection on these words, asking participants especially to ponder the difference between *saying* prayers and *being* prayers. What would it mean to *be* a prayer? After a minute of silence, invite brief responses.

- Continue with the passage from Norris, which relates this story:

  > I was at the beach, walking along the water's edge when a young child ran on very unsteady legs into the water. . . .
  >
  > His small body was intense with concentration. He was thrumming like an instrument, standing there in the water. Then he turned and, still deep in the experience, walked unsteadily out of the water and over the thin strip of pebbles at the water's edge. Then he made a kind of circle and went right back into the water up to his thighs for another experience of sea. He did this perhaps seven or eight times, as if verifying what this wet, cold living thing called water was to him.
  >
  > . . . Finally, fully satisfied, he stood in his wet diapers and began an unintelligible but eloquent speech to the water, to the gulls, to the sand, to the world. This baby was obviously not yet speaking with words, but he was certainly speaking with his heart.

> The sound was beautiful. He was tell-singing his experience with arms outflung. It was . . . a joyful noise to the Lord![2]

- Ask participants to ponder how this young child models for us *being* prayer. How does he express his experience of wonder and joy in this full moment of life? After a moment of quiet, again invite brief responses.

- Indicate that we will be learning how to recover something of this freedom to express what is in our hearts in ways other than words, a capacity we all knew as little children. Perhaps the image from this story will help us remember how to *become* prayer with all our body and soul.

- Sing or play a song. Suggestions:
  Contemporary: "Sacred the Body" (TFWS #2228; just reading the words together would be powerful and appropriate for the theme.)
  Taizé: "In the Lord I'll Be Ever Thankful" (TFWS #2195)

SHARING INSIGHTS (45 MINUTES)

Encourage group members to name ways they have experienced God's presence and guidance this week, especially in relation to the weekly reading and daily exercises. Remind them of this week's theme—discovering more fully the gift of our bodies in prayer.

1. Ask participants to briefly review the article and their journal entries for the week. *(5 minutes)*

2. Invite them to contribute their insights. As leader, model brevity and speaking your own truth by sharing your reflections first. Encourage deep listening to each person who shares, while fostering attention to God's wisdom in the sharing process. *(35 minutes)*

3. Conclude by asking the group to identify where they sensed the wisdom of the Holy Spirit in this sharing time. *(5 minutes)*

BREAK (10 MINUTES)

Post or prop the scripture texts at stations in each corner of the room.

DEEPER EXPLORATIONS (45 MINUTES)

Experiment with posture and movement as expressions of prayer.

Introduce the experience. (2 minutes)

Now that we have shared some of our experiences and feelings about our bodies in relation to prayer, we will practice embodied prayer a bit more and experiment together with physical gestures and postures that can help us to pray.

For the next ten minutes feel free to explore the four corners of the room, which represent four posture stations. At each station you will find a scripture text indicating a general posture of prayer. Spend some time letting yourself experience that prayer posture. You may try out all four stations or just one or two. Let yourself move into your own experience of prayer at each station; even though others may be near you, close your eyes and let your experience be your own.

Explore the posture stations. (10 minutes)

Station 1: "Lift up your hands to the holy place, and bless the LORD" (Ps. 134:2).

Station 2: "[Daniel] continued to go to his house, . . . and to get down on his knees three times a day to pray to his God and praise him" (Dan. 6:10).

Station 3: "But the tax collector . . . would not even look up to heaven, but was beating his breast and saying, 'God, be merciful to me, a sinner!'" (Luke 18:13). [A standing posture with hand over the heart and head bent]

Station 4: "Going a little farther, [Jesus] threw himself on the ground and prayed" (Matt. 26:39).

- After group members have explored the stations for eight minutes, give them a two-minute voice warning, then ring a bell or chime at the end of the ten minutes.

- Move chairs and table to one side of the room for this next process. If this would be easy to do yourself, you might do it quietly while group members are at the stations. If it will require help, do it quickly with several participants after ringing the chime.

Pray a psalm or the Lord's Prayer together. (10 minutes)

- Explain that now that you've "warmed up" with prayer postures, you will be praying a psalm (or the Lord's Prayer) with gesture and posture. Tell them you will read it three times, each time inviting them to step a bit further into embodiment. Remind them to take account of any physical limitations they may have and to participate as fully as they can without stressing themselves.

- Invite everyone to stand in a circle wide enough so each person has space to move freely.

- Before you read this first time, invite participants simply to *imagine* movements corresponding to the phrases and their feeling tones. Read, without rushing, the psalm verses or prayer you have chosen in advance.

- Before reading the second time, invite participants to close their eyes and use their hands and arms to express what they are hearing as you read. Read through it again at a slower pace with pauses between each phrase.

- Before reading the third time, ask everyone to open their eyes and let their whole body move in relation to the phrases they hear. Invite them to *feel* the psalm in their body. Read it a third time, leaving pauses between phrases.

Sculpt the psalm or prayer together. (10 minutes)

- While still in a circle, invite the group to "sculpt" your psalm or prayer now. Indicate a stage area for the sculpture around the person to your right in the circle. If you have enough participants relative to the number of verses, ask one volunteer to stand outside the process as a praying observer.

- Explain the process first: As you read the first verse, the first person in the circle will strike a pose or express a movement reminiscent of that verse. As you read the second verse, the next person will stand by the first with a pose/movement expressing that verse. Each person in the group will add a pose/movement to the sculpture until all stand clustered together. If there are more verses than persons in the group, the first several participants will continue with another pose/movement in the sculpture. As leader, you will add your movement to the group after reading the last verse. If there are fewer verses than participants, you and the remaining group members will prayerfully observe this dynamic sculpting process. Be sure everyone understands the basic idea.

- Now sculpt the psalm. Remind the group that this is a playful expression of prayer in which our bodies participate, helping us to pray with the whole of our being.

- When the sculpture is complete, invite everyone to hold the poses for a few moments, sensing the feel of the whole group in this form of prayer. As leader, say **Amen** when you are ready to release people from the formation. (The mood of this expression of prayer may vary widely from group to group. It may feel serious or humorous. Be prepared for laughter, expressions of surprise, or even tears.) [*Option:* Have your observer take a digital/instant photo of the sculpture before releasing the pose.]

Reflect with journal. (3 minutes)

Invite brief journal reflection on the experience of this form of prayer. Ask, **What was it like to include our bodies in prayer as** *a group*?

Share reflections. (10 minutes)

Share insights, feelings, and any new perspectives gained in this whole sequence of explorations into embodied prayer. If questions arise, encourage responses from others in the group. If you had observers, invite them to share their perspectives.

Reset chairs in a circle around the focus table.

Closing (10 minutes)

- Set on the focus table a basket filled with physical reminders of God's presence in all circumstances (small stones, pocket crosses, wrist/finger strings, tea candles). Light the Christ candle and invite the group into silence. (*Allow a minute or so.*)
- Ask all to get in touch with a challenging decision, meeting, task, or personal relationship that will have an impact on them within the coming week or so. (*Allow a minute.*)
- Invite participants to take several deep breaths. Encourage them to become aware of God's presence within their hearts and in the midst of all of life. (*Allow a minute.*)
- Now invite each person to choose a physical reminder of God's presence from the basket on the focus table. Take one yourself. When all have made their selections, point out that physical symbols are another aspect of embodied prayer. Ask them to ponder how they will use this physical sign as a reminder of divine grace and guidance in relation to the challenging situation they have identified. (*Allow a minute.*)
- Invite participants to offer one-sentence prayers of petition or praise.
- Sing a song or chant. Suggestion:

    Taizé: "Come and Fill Our Hearts " (TFWS #2157)

    Contemporary: "Lord of All Hopefulness" (TFWS #2197, URWB #179)
- Offer a benediction.

[Handwritten notes:]

Last Sunday "Prayer + Social transformation"
Ignatius + Nena Meimaris
Debbie Pugh
The possible reach of our prayers is Awesome.

Let's begin with prayer Now —
Father guide our thoughts as we study today —
Help us to listen so that we may hear
your Spirit speaking to us.

Week 7
Scriptural Prayer

PREPARATION

Prepare yourself spiritually. Read the article for Week 7; reflect on each daily exercise, and record your responses in your journal. Pray that the Holy Spirit will enlighten your reading of scripture and the way your group experiences God's Word in the weekly meeting. Familiarize yourself with the group process, and practice your timing on step 3 of the *lectio* with Ezekiel 37.

Take a few moments to visualize each person in your small group held in the vitality and radiance of Christ's life-giving love.

Prepare materials and the meeting space.

- Review the Weekly Needs at a Glance for items listed under All Meetings as well as those under this week's title, "Scriptural Prayer." Make a copy of the Ezekiel 37 reflection sheet for each participant and gather the other materials listed.
- Place the Christ candle centrally as a focal point for worship and sharing. Post the Candle Prayer and ground rules if you need them.
- Select songs and songbooks and/or recorded music to play.

Review the intent of this meeting: To discover as a group the richness of scripture, allowing others' insights into God's Word to deepen personal illumination and to build a corporate understanding.

OPENING (10 MINUTES)

Welcome all participants as they enter.

Set a context.

This is Week 7 of our ten-week journey through *The Way of Prayer*. While God's Word undergirds all our prayer, this week we will focus on how to pray the scriptures through *lectio divina* and the examen prayer. By doing this together, we discover how much richer the Bible can be when we hear the Spirit speaking to each and all of us through it.

Join together in worship.

- Light the Christ candle and recite the Candle Prayer, or offer a prayer such as this: **Holy Spirit, come, illumine our minds and hearts as we listen together for the Word of Life in this sacred text. Bring God close and help us know the presence of the living Christ among us. We ask it in his name. Amen.**

- Share the following quote from Thomas Kelly, reading slowly:

  Read your Bibles, and feel your way back into that Source and Spring of Life which bubbled up in the Bible-writers. And you'll find that Source and Spring of Life bubbling up *within you also*.[1]

- Invite your group to imagine the Source and Spring of Life as they listen to this passage:

  "Abide in me, as I abide in you. Just as the branch cannot bear fruit by itself unless it abides in the vine, neither can you unless you abide in me. I am the vine, you are the branches. Those who abide in me and I in them bear much fruit, because apart from me you can do nothing" (John 15:4-5).

- Ask participants to imagine themselves as branches in the vine of Christ, receiving the sap of God's own vitality, love, and joy through him. . . . . Invite them to get in touch with the rich soil of God's being in which the vine of Christ is deeply rooted. . . . Remind them that this is the Source and Spring of Life that nourished the writers of scripture. Invite them to allow that same Source to enter their minds and hearts in prayer now. . . . *(offer a minute of silence)*

- Invite brief sentence prayers of thanks and petition, ending with your own brief prayer.

- Close by singing or listening to a song. Suggestions:

  Traditional: "Blessed Jesus, at Thy Word" (UMH #596)

  Contemporary: "Thy Word Is a Lamp" (UMH #601)

  Taizé: "Come and Fill Our Hearts" (TFWS #2157, URWB #378)

SHARING INSIGHTS (45 MINUTES)

Encourage group members to name ways they have experienced God's presence and guidance this week, especially in relation to the weekly reading and daily exercises. Remind them of this week's theme—listening together to God's Word.

1. Let participants review the article and their journal entries for the week. *(5 minutes)*

2. Invite them to contribute their insights. As leader, model brevity and speaking your own truth by sharing your reflections first. Encourage deep listening to each person who shares, while paying attention to God's guidance in the sharing process. *(35 minutes)*

3. Conclude by asking the group to identify where they sensed the presence or guidance of the Spirit in this sharing time. *(5 minutes)*

BREAK (10 MINUTES)

DEEPER EXPLORATIONS (45 MINUTES)

Guide a group experience with lectio *and allow it to lead into a corporate prayer of examen.*

Introduce the experience. (1 minute) Pg 90-91   Monastic— Spiritual Rhythm

> We will be practicing group *lectio divina* with a text that continues to remind us of the need for God's Spirit in all matters of faith. In this process we will discover the value of hearing the Word reflected through the minds and hearts of our companions in the Spirit. The same text will guide us into a prayer of examen for our Closing today.

Practice lectio divina *with Ezekiel 37:1-14. (29 minutes)*

- Review the process of *lectio divina* on pages 90–91 of the Participant's Book. *(3 minutes)*

- Indicate that you will guide the group through a *lectio* process exploring Ezekiel 37:1-14, a prophetic vision commonly called "the valley of dry bones." Ask everyone to find space in the room he or she will find comfortable for the next twenty minutes or so. Be sure participants have their journals and Bibles with them. *(2 minutes)*

- Read the text and guide the group as follows:

Step 1: *lectio (4 minutes)*

> As I read these verses out loud for the first time, simply let the words wash over you. Pause over any words or phrases that capture your attention. Be alert to your senses. What sights, sounds, textures, tastes, and smells appear in this story? Read the text slowly. Pause for one minute. Then invite participants to record in their journals the words, phrases, or

impressions that stayed with them. Tell them it's not yet necessary to write or reflect on anything further. Pause another minute to allow for recording.

10:10 Step 2: *meditatio (10 minutes)* Reflect

Distribute copies of the "Reflection Sheet on Ezekiel 37" (page 70). Invite participants to read the prophecy from their Bibles, a few verses at a time, using the reflection sheet for their responses. They will have ten minutes for this meditation. At end of this time, ring a bell or chime. Pause to allow transition to the next step.

10:20 Step 3: *oratio (4 minutes, with 30-second pauses where indicated)* Respond

Let's now spend several minutes in prayer. Ask the Spirit to deepen your living encounter with God through this sacred text. You have already entered it with your imagination, but let your prayer carry you deeper into the mystery.

Begin by inviting God into the valley where your dry bones reside. Pray for breath. Pray for the Spirit to enter your bones. 30 Where do you perceive some of your "bones" coming together? 30 Which are quick to join up, and which seem slow? 30 Where do you feel most resistance to this movement of new life? 30 Open yourself to God as much as possible. Ask God for grace to receive the gift. 30 Thank God for the promise of new life and a new spirit. 30 Amen.

10:24 Step 4: *contemplatio (3 minutes)* Rest

Read verses 5 and 14 slowly again. Say, "Allow these words to rest deep within you. Sit silently in the presence of the God who brings life out of death. *(allow 2 minutes)*

10:27 Step 5: *incarnatio (3 minutes)* (one small action)

Read verses 9-10 a final time with emphasis on the word *prophesy.* Point out that the Spirit brings life, but God relies on the prophet to speak the words. Then ask, "What do you feel God calling you to say or do? How can you participate in God's project of renewing life? Think on this and record your ideas in your journal. Consider realistic goals and seek God's blessing for your plan. *(allow 2 minutes)*

10:30 *Share insights in triads. (10 minutes)*

Share in plenary. (5 minutes)

Capture key insights and reflections on this process from each triad. Reinforce the importance of this kind of meditation and prayer with scripture.

10:35 **CLOSING (10 MINUTES)**

Set the table: Place a few dry twigs or sticks on the worship table as a symbol of the dry bones. Have a small bowl of water with a single floating candle or fresh flower nearby but hidden from view.

Read again Ezekiel 37:1-3, 9-12. Remind the group that while it has personal application, this vision really concerns "a vast multitude"—the whole house of Israel, the people of God. So it would be true to the vision to consider our congregation(s) and larger church body in relation to this prophecy.

Spiritual Review of our lives

Invite participants to a group prayer of examen by reflecting prayerfully aloud on the following questions. Be sure to leave space for reflection and sharing after each question but indicate that not everyone needs to respond to each question, only those who feel moved to speak:

- *Examen of conscience:*

  Where do we see the valley of dry bones in the church?

  How do our personal dry bones relate to the larger picture of "death valley" in our churches?

  Where do we need to confess and repent?

- *Examen of consciousness:*

  Where has God's Spirit breathed new life into our churches?

  Where do we see evidence of grace, resurrection, and "the footprints of the holy"?

  For what can we offer praise and thanks?

Sing "Breathe on Me, Breath of God," first with "me/I" and then with "us/we." Remove the dry twigs and place the bowl of water with its floating candle or flower on the worship table as a sign of the new life God wants to give us.

Offer a benediction.

Lord, thank you for your Spirit here today. Continue to guide our thoughts and prayers. as we search for your truth Be with us and Pastor Julie in the worship service that follows. .... Amen.

Reflection Sheet on Ezekiel 37

Read each cluster of verses and respond on this sheet to the following questions. Use the back side if more space is needed.

1. Ezekiel 37:1-3. Of what do the dry bones remind you? Who do you know who has reached a dead end in their lives? What areas of your own life seem to have dried up and died? These are your own dry bones.

2. Ezekiel 37:4-10. Imagine the living Spirit of God breathing into you. Begin to feel your dry bones rattling and coming together. What are the sinews on your bones like? What kind of skin covers them? What does it mean for your dry bones to receive breath and live? Picture all this, and write or draw the vision below.

3. Ezekiel 37:11-14. The dry bones, now living, are ready to emerge from their grave. How will you let God bring forth the parts of your life that you thought had dried up and died?

Week 8
Contemplative Prayer

PREPARATION

Prepare yourself spiritually. Read the article for Week 8; reflect on each daily exercise; and record responses in your journal. Be sure to complete Exercise 4 so that you have a personal experience with Centering Prayer before guiding the group through it. Pray for the grace to be a clear, gentle, and effective leader within the group. Pray also that each participant might be drawn to a deeper experience of God's reality through contemplative prayer and that their practice of contemplation would increase openness to divine mystery and trust in God's goodness.

Prepare materials and the meeting space.
- Refer to Weekly Needs at a Glance, briefly reviewing items listed under All Meetings, as well as this week's title, "Contemplative Prayer."
- Arrange chairs in a circle or around a table with the Christ candle in the center.
- If appropriate, have the Candle Prayer and ground rules posted for all to see.
- Familiarize yourself with the group process of the weekly meeting.
- Select songs for the Opening and Closing and recorded instrumental music for Closing.

Review the intent of the meeting: To share questions and insights about contemplative prayer, and to experience as a group this least familiar form of Christian prayer.

OPENING (10 MINUTES)

Welcome all participants as they enter.

Set a context.

As we near the end of our exploration of *The Way of Prayer*, we find ourselves this week sampling the most mysterious and least familiar form of Christian prayer, contemplation. Today we will have an opportunity to share our thoughts and experiences with this form of prayer and to practice Centering Prayer as a group.

Join together in worship.

- Enter a spirit of worship by lighting the candle at the center of your group. Recite together the Candle Prayer, or offer words such as these: **May the light of Christ reveal to us God's constant presence and love, inviting us to enter the Presence, absorb God's love, and reflect it back with all our heart. Amen.**

- Read Psalm 84:1-2. Read it slowly, savoring the words as you speak. After a few moments of quiet, invite participants to let these words connect them to their heart's deep desire for God, to *feel* their yearning, to stretch toward the joy of God's presence. Read the verses again with a little more pause between phrases. *(Leave a minute of silence after the second reading.)*

- Read the following promise, written by the devotional writer Thomas Kelly:

  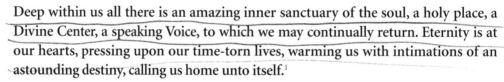
  > Deep within us all there is an amazing inner sanctuary of the soul, a holy place, a Divine Center, a speaking Voice, to which we may continually return. Eternity is at our hearts, pressing upon our time-torn lives, warming us with intimations of an astounding destiny, calling us home unto itself.[1]

- Indicate that entering this inner sanctuary where we "breathe the atmosphere of Eternity" (Evelyn Underhill's phrase) is the essence of contemplative prayer.

- Sing "Sanctuary" (TFWS #2164) two or three times quietly as a prayer. Many participants will be familiar with this song even if you do not have music available ("Lord, prepare me to be a sanctuary . . .")

  Other song options: "Come and Find the Quiet Center" (TFWS #2128), "Be Still and Know That I Am God" (TFWS #2057), "Without Seeing You" (TFWS #2206)

SHARING INSIGHTS (45 MINUTES)

Encourage participants to name ways they have experienced God's presence this past week, especially in relation to the reading and daily exercises. Remind them of the theme—opening to the mystery of God's presence and trusting God's grace through contemplative prayer.

1. Ask participants to review the article and their journal entries for this week. *(5 minutes)*

2. Invite them to contribute their insights. As leader, model the sharing by offering your own brief reflections first. Encourage deep and active listening. *(35 minutes)*

3. Invite the group to identify any common themes or refrains that you heard during the sharing. Ask, **What might the Spirit be saying to us through these refrains?** *(5 minutes)*

BREAK (10 MINUTES)

DEEPER EXPLORATIONS (45 MINUTES)

Guide the group in practicing the presence of God together through Centering Prayer.

Set a context. (1 minute)

Centering Prayer is a helpful contemporary form of contemplative prayer. The basic method is easy to learn and can be practiced individually. But many people find Centering Prayer easier to sustain over time when they practice it in a group setting. We will practice it today as a group. Perhaps it will be a form of prayer some would like to continue in a group after we have completed *The Way of Prayer.*

Introduce Centering Prayer time. (14 minutes)

- Ground this way of prayer firmly in the biblical tradition by referring to these passages:
  1. "Be still, and know that I am God!" (Ps. 46:10).
  2. "'Go into your room and shut the door and pray to your Father who is in secret'" (Matt. 6:6).
  3. "'You shall love the Lord your God with all your heart, and with all your soul, and with all your mind'" (Matt. 22:37).

Point out that Centering Prayer provides a way to fulfill all three imperatives. It is a form of stillness, secret prayer, love, and pure adoration.

- Remind participants of the basic process of Centering Prayer. Refer to the summary page in the Participant's Book, page 106.

- Read Philippians 2:5-7a. Use this passage to help interpret what we do in Centering Prayer: **We are called to imitate the self-emptying of Christ. This may be a helpful way to think of offering God our distractions in prayer. We empty ourselves of distractions over and over, just as Jesus emptied himself to be fully available to God.**

- Suggest options from scripture for the prayer word, such as: *Adonai, Lord, Glory, Light, Peace, Beloved, Holy, Love, Shekinah.*

- Respond as best you can to questions that may arise.

Guide a time of Centering Prayer. (20 minutes)

- Invite group members to go anywhere they wish within sound range of your chime. Ask them to settle peacefully in a comfortable position.

- Use a soft chime sound to signal both the beginning and end of prayer time. You may shorten the time to fifteen minutes, based on the experience level of the group members.

- Allow participants a minute or so after the ending chime to come back fully into the room, physically and mentally.

Debrief the experience. (10 minutes)

- Give all a chance, if they choose, to say a few words about their experience of this way of prayer. Begin by focusing on how they experienced the process.

- Respond to questions that are likely to arise. See the Leader's Note on page 75 of this Leader's Guide for Frequently Asked Questions (FAQs) and responses.

CLOSING (10 MINUTES)

- Take a moment to get quiet together, remembering God's loving presence. *(1 minute)*

- Create a prayer sound. *(3 minutes)*

    Explain that while Centering Prayer is about silence, our closing prayer is about sound. Invite the group to create a contemplative sound by repeating their prayer words aloud all together for about a minute.

    Repeat your prayer word at a comfortable pace, and listen to the sound of the whole group praying. We'll start whispering our prayer word softly, and allow the Spirit to move us to swell or quiet the volume. Let's begin now by taking two slow breaths; then we'll start speaking our words and listening to the sound of our prayer.

    As leader, track timing and strike chime softly to signal the end of the prayer sound.

- Sing "Come and Fill Our Hearts" (TFWS #2157). *(2–3 minutes)*

    Short repeated songs and chants create contemplative space and can lead us into prayerful communion with God. Let's pray through the means of chant for a few minutes, letting the Spirit move our timing. (Sing through at least four to five times)

Option: Hum together your special group song or another favorite song; no words.

• Play quiet instrumental music and invite everyone to slowly breathe their prayer word in silence as they listen. *(2 minutes)*

• Offer a benediction.

• Explain next week's Deeper Explorations. Readiness to guide the group in prayer will require giving special attention to Exercise 5. Tell the group how much time each person will have, dividing thirty-five minutes by the number in your group (be sure to include yourself). Participants will say a few words about why they chose this particular form of prayer, so they will need to factor in this time as well.

Leader's Note
Frequently Asked Questions

Q: **Is Centering Prayer a form of contemplative prayer?**

A: Yes and no. True contemplative prayer is a grace given by the Holy Spirit. Centering Prayer is a method that helps prepare us to receive the gift of contemplation. It moves us beyond conversation to communion with God.

Q: **Is the sacred word repeated continually like phrases of a breath prayer?**

A: No. The prayer word is a symbol of our intention and desire to be in God's holy, loving presence. We use it to remind ourselves to rest in God's presence and consent to the Spirit's action within us. It is only repeated when we find ourselves distracted from this purpose by our thoughts.

Q: **What if I'm not good at this kind of prayer?**

A: There is no "good" or "bad" in this kind of prayer. We avoid analyzing or judging our experience when practicing Centering Prayer. We are not aiming at a certain kind of experience like having no thoughts or becoming peaceful. We are not seeking spiritual insights or healing. We are taking time to be in God's presence and staying open to what God may choose to do in and with us.

For more information, go to www.centeringprayer.com

Praying with and for Others

PREPARATION

Prepare yourself spiritually. Read the article for Week 9; reflect on each of the daily exercises, and record your responses in your journal. Give particular attention to Exercise 5 so that you, alongside other participants, are prepared to guide the group in a specific way of prayer during the Deeper Explorations. Ponder how you would like to be present as leader in these last two group meetings of *The Way of Prayer*. Pray that the community dimension of prayer might be deeply impressed on each participant's heart and bear fruit for building God's reign in the larger communities of family, church, neighborhood, nation, and world.

Prepare materials and the meeting space.

- Refer to Weekly Needs at a Glance, briefly reviewing items listed under All Meetings as well as this week's title, "Praying with and for Others." You will need a small container for anointing oil or an oil button (solidified oil in small round container with a screw-on lid, available in some religious supply stores).
- Arrange chairs in a circle or around a table with the Christ candle in the center.
- Select songs and/or recorded music for the Opening and Closing.

Review the intent of the meeting: To share the meaning of prayer in and for community and to experience a variety of ways to pray together that have become meaningful to members of this *Companions* community.

OPENING (10 MINUTES)

Welcome all participants as they enter.

Set a context.

Welcome to Week 9 of our explorations in *The Way of Prayer*. As we near the conclusion of this small-group experience, we will be sharing perspectives on prayer in community and guiding one another in ways of prayer that have become meaningful to us over the course of our time together. Let's encourage one another to reflect on ways to continue praying with and for the others beyond the time frame of this group experience.

Join together in worship.

- Enter a spirit of worship by lighting the candle at the center of your group. Recite together the Candle Prayer, or offer words such as these:

> Blessed Trinity of Love,
> God whose essence is community:
> May we begin to grasp
> what it means to be grasped by your love
> and participate in your life.
> In the spirit of Christ we pray. Amen.

- Read Psalm 133. After a pause, repeat verses 1 and 3. Allow a little time to absorb the words.

- Read the following quote from Jean Vanier, founder of the L'Arche Community (a residential faith community for persons with mental and physical limitations):

> The longer we journey on the road to unity, the more the sense of belonging grows and deepens. The sense is not just one of belonging to a community. It is a sense of belonging to the universe, to the earth, to the air, to the water, to everything that lives, to all humanity.[1]

- After a minute of quiet, invite sentence prayers of praise, thanksgiving, and supplication.

- Close with a song. Suggestions:

  Traditional: "We Are One in the Spirit" (also titled "They'll Know We Are Christians by Our Love") (TFWS #2223)

  Contemporary: "We Are the Body of Christ" (TFWS #2227) or "We Are One in Christ Jesus" ("Somos Uno en Cristo") (TFWS #2229)

SHARING INSIGHTS (45 MINUTES)

Encourage group members to name ways in which they have experienced God's presence this past week, especially in relation to the reading and daily exercises. Remind them of the theme—praying with and for others.

1. Ask participants to review the article and their journal entries for this week. *(5 minutes)*

2. Invite them to contribute their insights, saving responses to Exercise 5 for the Deeper Explorations. Model the sharing by offering your own brief reflections first. Encourage deep and active listening to others and to God. *(35 minutes)*

3. Invite others to identify common themes or refrains heard during this sharing. Ask what the Spirit might be saying to us through these common themes. *(5 minutes)*

BREAK (10 MINUTES)

DEEPER EXPLORATIONS (45 MINUTES)

Give each participant an opportunity to lead the group in a form of shared prayer.

Set a context. (1 minute)

> **This second half of our meeting gives time for each of us in turn to guide the group through a chosen form of prayer that may have special significance for us. Remember that the purpose of this time is to enhance and strengthen our common prayer life.**

Introduce the time of shared leadership. (4 minutes)

Read Colossians 1:9-12, inviting participants to look at this passage in their own Bibles as you read. Ask them to identify what Paul and Timothy are praying for in the Colossian church (knowledge of God's will, spiritual wisdom/understanding, lives worthy of the Lord, fruitful works, spiritual strength, patient endurance, joyful thanks). List these on newsprint.

Ask participants to identify their deep prayers for this *Companions* group—what are the larger spiritual gifts they hope this small community will receive from these weeks together? List these also on newsprint and place the two lists side by side.

> **Over the next thirty-five minutes, we will take turns leading the group in the form of prayer that we chose and developed in Exercise 5. The purpose is to share something of what we have learned concerning various ways of prayer and to enhance and strengthen the prayer life of our small-group community.**

Lead one another in various expressions of prayer. (35 minutes)

- Remind the group of approximately how much time each person has to lead, acknowledging that some may take less time and some more.

- Invite each one to begin by telling briefly why he or she selected this form of prayer for the group and what it means personally.

- Suggest a moment of quiet, then pray aloud for the Spirit to guide the group.

- Invite anyone who would like to go first to do so; if no one volunteers, lead first yourself.

Reflect on the experience. (5 minutes)

Ask what it has been like to be guided through these various forms of prayer. You might use questions like these: **What has spoken to your heart? Did we as a group sense a stronger common bond through any particular prayer form? What prayer forms will you continue?**

CLOSING (10 MINUTES)

- Read Colossians 3:16-17. Remind the group that even in the early church Christians dwelled in Christ's word and prayer in community in a rich variety of ways. Affirm the ways you have experienced this richness today.

- Invite the group into a time of spontaneous prayers of thanksgiving (for persons in this group, for gifts of leadership, for the Spirit's guidance). Close by praying together "The Prayer of Saint Francis" (page 117, Participant's Book), using *us* and *we*.

- Anoint each person in your group with oil, offering the following blessing:

  May you remain faithful in your personal prayer;

  may you find strength in praying with your community of faith;

  and may you bring your gifts of leadership to others as God leads you. Amen.

- Say or sing a blessing.

- Instruct the group to be sure to complete Exercise 5 of the coming week in preparation for the closing meeting.

Week 10
Prayer and Social Transformation

PREPARATION

Prepare yourself spiritually. Read the article for Week 10; reflect on each of the daily exercises, and record your responses in your journal. Be sure to complete Exercise 5 so you are prepared to participate in the Closing alongside your companions. Pray for the grace to be a clear, open vessel of God's wisdom and love within the group. Pray also that each participant might find blessing in this gathering for closure to the small-group experience, as well as inspiration and energy to carry on faithfully with a life of prayer both personally and in community.

Prepare materials and the meeting space.

- Refer to Weekly Needs at a Glance, reviewing items listed under All Meetings as well as this week's title, "Prayer and Social Transformation." Familiarize yourself with the Deeper Explorations process. Note that preparing materials will take more time than usual this week. Specifically:

  1. You will need to locate magazines with pictures of human and natural interest depicting or suggesting images of harmony, health, peace, and vitality in social, economic, political, and ecological realms. You will want to clip these out and save them in a folder or envelope for the Deeper Explorations.

  2. You will also need to create a large circle (at least four feet in diameter) of heavy paper or cardboard and mark it with wedge lines leaving a smaller (six- to eight-inch) circle empty at the center. Suggestion: If you have eight or fewer in your group, create a wedge for each person. If you have more than eight you may assign two participants to some of the wedges, or create a larger circle and divide it into the number of persons in your group (remember to include yourself).

- Arrange chairs in a circle or around a table with the Christ candle in the center. For the Deeper Explorations you will need a table large enough to hold the mandala (the large cirlce comprised of wedges), as well as space for magazine pictures and art supplies to be spread out.

- Select songs and recorded music for the Opening and Closing.

Review the intent of the meeting: To ponder with one another the mystery of prayer and social transformation and to envision together the reality of God's future reign.

OPENING (10 MINUTES)

Welcome all participants as they enter.

Set a context.

> Welcome to our final week in this small-group experience with *The Way of Prayer*. We have explored many rich possibilities of prayer, expanding our repertoire of methods and enlarging our understanding of how God works with us and within us. Today we will look at the relationship of prayer to God's great work of bringing the divine reign to fruition among us. This aim was central to Jesus' life purpose and teaching: helping us perceive the in-breaking of the kingdom of God and urging us to live in light of God's reign by the grace of the Spirit.

Join together in worship.

- Enter a spirit of worship by lighting the candle at the center of your group. Recite together the Candle Prayer, or offer words such as these:

> The light of Christ shines in the darkness.
> The darkness has not overcome it.
> As we stay focused on the light of Christ,
> the darkness shall not overcome us.
> May we be patient and faithful in prayer,
> trusting God's timing and transforming grace.
> Thanks be to God,
> who has given us the victory through our Lord Jesus Christ! Amen.

- Read the following verses from the letter of James:

> Be doers of the word, and not merely hearers who deceive themselves. . . . What good is it, my brothers and sisters, if you say you have faith but do not have works? . . . For

just as the body without the spirit is dead, so faith without works is also dead" (1:22; 2:14, 26).

- *After a pause, read the following quote from William Law (1686–1761, English spiritual writer):*

  As actions are of much more significance than words, it must be a much more acceptable worship to glorify God in all the actions of our common life than with any little form of words at any particular times.[1]

- Invite reflection on these two readings in relation to the idea that our faithful actions can be expressions of prayer. Ask participants to ponder whether they have experienced or sensed this truth in their lives at some point. Allow a minute of silence, then invite two or three group members to share briefly if they choose.

- Voice a short prayer that summarizes the theme of prayer and action in relation to God's reign.

- Close by singing or playing a recorded song. Suggestions:

  Traditional: "O Spirit of the Living God" (UMH #539) or "Where Charity and Love Prevail" (UMH #549)

  Contemporary: "For One Great Peace" (TFWS #2185) or "Make Me a Servant" (TFWS #2176)

SHARING INSIGHTS (45 MINUTES)

Encourage group members to name ways in which they have experienced God's presence this past week. Remind them of the theme—to ponder with each other the mystery of prayer and social transformation, and to envision together the reality of God's future reign.

1. Ask participants to review the article and their journal entries for this week. *(5 minutes)*

2. Invite them to contribute their insights, saving responses to Exercise 5 for the Deeper Explorations. You may wish to model sharing by offering your own brief reflections first. Encourage deep and active listening to others and to God. *(35 minutes)*

3. Identify together any common themes or refrains that you heard in this sharing. Ask what the Spirit might be communicating to us through these themes. *(5 minutes)*

BREAK (10 MINUTES)

DEEPER EXPLORATIONS (45 MINUTES)

Imagine together the basic contours and characteristics of God's new creation.

Set a context. (2 minutes)

> We often think of God's kingdom as a future hope, but Jesus counsels his followers to perceive the nearness of God's reign even now. In fact, he embodies the reign of God in his own being. He is the new creation, the promised restoration of life as God intends.
>
> So, as a way to bring together what we've been learning and practicing about prayer, we are going to envision together the shape and character of this new creation. What does the life of the risen Christ look like in our world today, and what can it look like? If "intercessors . . . believe the future into being," as Walter Wink says, our prayer today can be part of this creative effort. May God bless our thinking and imagining and inspire our participation in the gracious reign of God.

Introduce the theme of new creation. (10 minutes)

- Read 2 Corinthians 5:17: "If anyone is in Christ, there is a new creation."
- Invite four group members to read, in turn, Romans 8:18-25; Galatians 3:25-28; Romans 12:9-21; and Colossians 3:12-15. Ask participants to listen carefully to each passage for words, phrases, or images that describe the reign of God in our midst or that suggest characteristics of the promised new creation in Christ. They may wish to mark and read each text in their own Bibles. After each text is read, allow a minute of silence, then ask for responses and list them on newsprint.
- Invite participants to name other scripture passages that speak to them of new creation.

Imagine the future into being. (8 minutes)

- Indicate that we will now be exercising our imaginations to envision the New Creation. Invite participants to get out their journals. Ask: **What is our role—your role—in helping to create the reign of God? How can we cooperate in bringing about God's best intention for the earth and all its people and creatures? How might we participate in God's vision for life in this world?**
- Suggest that all refer to the newsprint list to remind themselves of characteristics of God's reign they want to participate in more fully, and invite prayerful consideration.
- Allow six to seven minutes for personal journaling.

Picture the new creation together. (15 minutes)

- Invite participants to take paper, colored pencils or markers, scissors, magazine clippings, and glue sticks from the table where you have laid them out.
- Ask everyone to create symbols for the New Creation by drawing colors, images, or word pictures. They can incorporate magazine pictures if they wish. *(10 minutes)*
- Share the symbols in the group. Ask how they differ and what they have in common.

Create a group mandala. (10 minutes)

- Explain that a mandala is an image of wholeness and integration, a good symbol for the reign of God. (See Leader's Note, page 86 for more background on mandalas).
- On a table lay out the large circle of heavy paper or cardboard marked with one wedge for each person in your group. (If you have a larger group, you might assign two persons to a wedge.) Invite all to work together around the circle, finding ways to get their personal symbols onto each wedge using scissors and glue. This is a brief process so they will need to work quickly; it does not need to look perfect! *(5 minutes)*
- Now invite the group to find a common symbol or design signifying the new creation to place in the small empty circle at the center of the mandala. *(2–3 minutes)*
- Step back to look together at the creation. Take a moment to note insights or wonderings.

CLOSING (10 MINUTES)

- Place the group mandala where it is visible to all for closing worship.
- Light the Christ candle again if it was extinguished earlier.
- Remind participants of Exercise 5 of this final week. Read again the three questions everyone had a chance to respond to in three to four sentences to be shared with the group.
- Give everyone a chance to locate those sentences, and invite the sharing to begin. Be sure all have an opportunity to offer thoughts, hopes, and prayers for the group.
- Enter into a time of prayer: Begin with a moment of silence, then invite prayers of thanksgiving and prayers for the future of this small community in relation to family, church, and world.
- Sing or play a song of celebration and commitment. Suggestions:
  Traditional: "Many Gifts, One Spirit" (UMH #114)
  Contemporary: "The Summons" (TFWS #2130)
- Offer a benediction. (You might consider reading or paraphrasing Ephesians 3:14-21.)

Leader's Note
Background on Mandalas

The mandala is a universal image of wholeness, totality, and centering. The word literally means "to be in possession of one's essence." People in all times and cultures have created such images to represent their inner reality.

We carry within us, at the center of our being, a sanctuary, a holy place where the human and divine meet. People of faith call it the soul. We have the imprint of our own wholeness embedded in us and a basic instinct to make it real (to realize it). For Christians, Christ is the wholeness of our soul, the divine image in all its glory that we too are becoming. The "Rose Windows" of great cathedrals are mandalas, images of cosmic wholeness and invitations to contemplate the deep center of our lives in God.

Creating a mandala is a way to center ourselves in prayer. A mandala can be considered a "picture of the soul" in any given time or circumstance. It can also symbolize the beauty and order of God's reign within and among us. Generally circular, the design always has a clear center and a well-marked boundary. It embodies a sense of order and balance, and helps to concentrate the energy of our prayer. Below is a sample mandala.

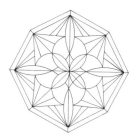

Notes

Preparatory Meeting

1. Eugene H. Peterson, *Working the Angles: The Shape of Pastoral Integrity* (Grand Rapids, Mich.: William B. Eerdmans, 1987), 103–4.

Week 1: How Do You Pray?

1. Edward Farrell, *Prayer Is a Hunger* (Denville, N.J.: Dimension Books, 1972), 23.

Week 2: Images of God

1. Calvin Miller, *Leadership* (Colorado Springs, Colo.: NavPress, 1987), 33.

Week 3: Praying by Heart

1. Thomas R. Kelly, *A Testament of Devotion* (San Francisco: HarperSanFrancisco, 1992), 76.
2. Dietrich Bonhoeffer, *Psalms: The Prayer Book of the Bible*, trans. James H. Burtness (Minneapolis, Minn.: Augsburg Publishing House, 1970), 21.
3. Ron DelBene, *Into the Light: A Simple Way to Pray with the Sick and the Dying* (Nashville, Tenn.: Upper Room Books, 1988), 32. The first paragraph of these notes is adapted from this book.

Week 5: Praying by Gaze

1. Henri J. M. Nouwen, *Clowning in Rome: Reflections on Solitude, Celibacy, Prayer, and Contemplation* (Garden City, N.Y.: Image Books, 1979), 78.
2. Ibid.
3. Ibid., 106.
4. Gunilla Norris, *Being Home: A Book of Meditations* (New York: Crown Publishers, 1991), 60–61.

Week 6: Praying with Our Bodies

1. Norris, *Being Home*, xix.
2. Ibid., xix–xx.

Week 7: Scriptural Prayer

1. Thomas R. Kelly, *The Eternal Promise* (London: Hodder and Stoughton, 1966), 103.

WEEK 8: CONTEMPLATIVE PRAYER

1. Kelly, *A Testament of Devotion*, 9.

WEEK 9: PRAYING WITH AND FOR OUR BODIES

1. Jean Vanier, *Community and Growth: Our Pilgrimage Together* (New York: Paulist Press, 1979), 4.

WEEK 10: PRAYER AND SOCIAL TRANSFORMATION

1. William Law, *A Serious Call to a Devout and Holy Life,* in *Total Devotion to God: Selected Writings of William Law*, ed. Keith Beasley-Topliffe (Nashville, Tenn.: Upper Room Books, 2000), 32.

Evaluation

When your group has completed *The Way of Prayer* resource, share your insights and experiences. Copy this page if you prefer not to tear it out. Use additional paper if needed.

1. Describe your group's experience with *The Way of Prayer*.

2. In what ways did the resource lead participants to a fuller understanding of spiritual formation and to a more experiential knowledge of spiritual practices?

   Please share your perceptions with us in this evaluation or through the discussion room at **www.companionsinchrist.org**.

3. What would improve *The Way of Prayer*?

4. Do you have follow-up plans for your group? If you have not already completed it, do you plan to begin the twenty-eight-week *Companions in Christ* foundational course or several of its parts?

5. What other kinds of resources are you looking for? What other topics would you like to see in the Companions in Christ series?

Mail to: Companions in Christ
c/o Editorial Director
Upper Room Ministries
P. O. Box 340004
Nashville, TN 37203-0004
Or FAX 615-340-1783

About the Author

Marjorie J. Thompson has worked closely with all facets of *Companions in Christ* from its origins. Designing the foundational twenty-eight-week resource, writing articles and leader guides for various titles in the Companions series, and training *Companions* trainers, she has helped to guide and shape this small-group ministry over a number of years.

Marjorie brings over twenty-five years of experience with retreat work, teaching, and writing in the area of Christian spiritual formation to her work as Director of Pathways in Congregational Spiritualtiy with Upper Room Ministries. She is the author of *Soul Feast: An Invitation to the Christian Spiritual Life* (Westminster/John Knox Press 1995/2005) and *Family, The Forming Center: A Vision of the Role of Family in Spiritual Formation* (Upper Room Books, 1996). An ordained minister in the Presbyterian Church USA, she has served in pastoral ministry and as adjunct instructor in several seminary settings. Marjorie's educational path includes Swarthmore College, McCormick Theological Seminary, and a Research Fellowship at Yale Divinity School where she was deeply influenced by her mentor, Henri J.M. Nouwen.